SUMMARY OF THE RIVER OF GLORY

52 Keys to Living in God's Presence

JODY KECK

DESTINY IMAGE

Destiny Image P.O. Box 310, Shippensburg, PA 17257-0310

This book and all other Destiny Image's books are available at Christian bookstores and distributors worldwide.

For Worldwide Distribution.

Reach us on the Internet: www.destinyimage.com.

ISBN 13 TP: 9798881501600

ISBN 13 eBook: 9798881501617

CONTENTS

INTRODUCTION

The River of Glory takes readers on a profound journey into the heart of spiritual intimacy, calling believers to encounter the depths of God's love, power, and presence. This summary encapsulates the book's powerful keys, guiding each of us toward living in God's river of glory—a life overflowing with His Spirit, holiness, and divine purpose. Through testimonies of miraculous encounters and personal transformation, the author offers not only a glimpse into God's supernatural realm but also a practical roadmap for embracing a life marked by His presence.

The book's teachings remind us that each believer is invited to dwell continually in God's glory, becoming a vessel through which His power flows. In these pages, readers will discover the transformative keys of prayer, holiness, and trust, designed to deepen their walk with the Lord. From understanding the true power of the Holy Spirit to embracing patience, sacrifice, and fruitfulness, the lessons shared are intended to equip and inspire believers to step into a greater alignment with God's will.

One central theme throughout the book is the believer's choice: to live either immersed in God's river or to drift aimlessly through life. *The River of Glory* challenges us to move beyond a superficial faith and embrace a relationship with God that is vibrant and unwavering. Each chapter serves as a reminder that the pursuit of God's presence is a lifelong journey, inviting readers to be transformed "from glory to glory." As we venture into the profound truths in *The River of Glory*, may our lives reflect His light and bring hope to a world longing for Him.

CHAPTER 1

BEGINNING

Bible Verse

Psalms 46:4 (NIV) - "There is a river whose streams make glad the city of God, the holy place where the Most High dwells."

Introduction

This chapter delves into the profound experiences of God's glory, tracing from historical figures like Moses to the present-day believer's desire to encounter God intimately. It describes the glory of God as a life-transforming presence that offers a deep sense of purpose, renewal, and intense emotional experiences to those who seek Him earnestly.

Word of Wisdom

"Moses went up the mountain; Israel did not have their own revelation. We need our own revelation and encounter! I

have gone up the mountain too, and am humbled and thrilled to share some of my personal encounters." Jody Keck

Main Theme

The chapter explores the multifaceted aspects of God's glory, emphasizing its role in providing spiritual renewal, purpose, and profound joy to believers, facilitating direct encounters with the divine through scriptural narratives and personal testimonies.

Key Points

- God's glory is a radiant manifestation of His divine attributes, bringing awe and reverence to those who witness it.
- Isaiah's vision of God in the temple reveals the overwhelming holiness and majesty of God's presence.
- Personal encounters with God's glory bring deep transformation and a sense of divine destiny.
- Revelations and spiritual insights often come in symbolic, profound experiences as shown through dreams and visions.
- The Holy Spirit plays a crucial role in sustaining believers with living water, symbolized by the river of life.
- Pursuing personal revelations and encounters with God is essential for spiritual growth and understanding.

Key Themes

- **Divine Encounters Transform:** Encountering God's glory transforms believers by offering a clearer sense of purpose and destiny, drawing them into deeper communion with God. This transformative experience is both a personal journey and a communal invitation to live in alignment with God's divine plan.
- **Historical and Personal Revelations:** The chapter bridges historical accounts, like those of Moses and Isaiah, with personal stories to illustrate that encounters with God's glory are not confined to the past but are accessible to all who seek Him earnestly today.
- **Symbolic Revelations:** Through vivid descriptions of dreams and prophetic symbols, the chapter emphasizes that God often communicates in ways that require spiritual discernment and readiness to understand deeper truths, encouraging believers to seek and interpret these divine messages.
- **Role of the Holy Spirit:** The Holy Spirit is depicted as the giver of life and the sustainer of believers, offering refreshment and renewal through His presence. This ongoing engagement is crucial for believers to remain vibrant and spiritually nourished.
- **Application of Spiritual Insights:** The chapter advocates for applying the insights gained from divine encounters in everyday life, suggesting that such applications can

lead to significant spiritual growth and fulfillment.

Conclusion

In the glory of God, believers find the ultimate source of life and joy. This chapter encourages readers to seek personal revelations and engage deeply with the spiritual dimensions of their faith, promising that such pursuits will lead to transformative experiences and a deeper understanding of God's purposes. As believers cultivate these encounters, they are promised a more profound experience of God's presence and an increased capacity to navigate life's challenges with divine guidance and wisdom.

CHAPTER 2

BORN AGAIN

Bible Verse

John 3:3 (ESV) - "Truly, truly, I say to you, unless one is born again he cannot see the kingdom of God."

Introduction

This chapter narrates the transformative journey of the author's father from a life marked by abuse and atheism to a profound spiritual awakening and conversion. It underscores the power of persistent prayer and the life-changing impact of encountering the Gospel and choosing to follow Jesus Christ.

Word of Wisdom

"Never underestimate the power of prayer. At 67 years of age, the skeptic had now become a believer!" Jody Keck

. . .

Main Theme

The central theme focuses on the concept of being 'born again' as a radical, personal transformation that aligns one's life with God's purposes, facilitated by acknowledging Jesus Christ as Lord and Savior and experiencing the renewing work of the Holy Spirit.

Key Points

- Personal transformation through being born again is a profound spiritual rebirth.
- Persistent prayer plays a crucial role in the conversion of others.
- The Holy Spirit is instrumental in softening hearts and guiding new believers.
- Water baptism is an essential follow-up to a profession of faith.
- A born-again life involves a radical shift in thoughts, emotions, and desires.
- True conversion introduces a person to a lifelong journey of faith and communion with God.

Key Themes

- **Transformative Power of the Gospel:** The Gospel's power to transform lives is vividly illustrated through the personal story of the author's father, who turned from atheism and abuse to embrace faith in Jesus, highlighting the Gospel's ability to change even the most hardened hearts.

- **Persistent Intercession:** The chapter emphasizes the importance of persistent, faith-filled prayer for the salvation of loved ones, illustrating that intercessory prayer can prepare hearts to receive the Gospel and lead to miraculous conversions, regardless of past beliefs or actions.
- **Role of the Holy Spirit in Conversion:** It describes how the Holy Spirit works to soften hearts towards repentance and faith, playing a critical role in the process of becoming born again and continuing to guide individuals in their new faith journey.
- **Significance of Baptism:** Baptism is portrayed as a pivotal step of obedience and a public declaration of new faith, symbolizing the washing away of the old life and the beginning of the new life in Christ.
- **Lifelong Spiritual Growth:** Following a conversion, there is a significant transformation in a believer's life that includes a new way of thinking and acting, which is nurtured through continuous spiritual disciplines like prayer, Bible study, and fellowship

Conclusion

Being born again is not merely a one-time event but the beginning of a lifelong journey of faith and transformation. This chapter invites readers to experience this new birth, offering hope and assurance of eternal life through Jesus Christ. It calls on readers to open their hearts to the radical change that comes with true repentance and faith, promising an eternal and fulfilling relationship with God.

CHAPTER 3

GIFTS OF THE SPIRIT

Bible Verse

1 Corinthians 12:8-10 (NIV) - "To one there is given through the Spirit a message of wisdom, to another a message of knowledge by means of the same Spirit, to another faith by the same Spirit, to another gifts of healing by that one Spirit, to another miraculous powers, to another prophecy, to another distinguishing between spirits, to another speaking in different kinds of tongues, and to still another the interpretation of tongues."

Introduction

This chapter recounts a moving experience at a church service in West Virginia where the manifestation of the Holy Spirit's gifts profoundly impacted attendees, particularly highlighting a miraculous healing of a woman from a wheelchair.

Word of Wisdom

"Jesus honors our faith at the level we can use it." Jody Keck

Main Theme

The chapter explores the diverse and powerful gifts of the Holy Spirit, which are given to believers to edify the church and demonstrate God's power through miraculous healings, prophecy, wisdom, and more.

Key Points

- The Holy Spirit imparts a variety of spiritual gifts to believers.
- These gifts include wisdom, knowledge, faith, healing, miracles, prophecy, discernment, tongues, and interpretation of tongues.
- Spiritual gifts are intended for the edification of the church and the glorification of God.
- Personal testimonies of miracles can bolster faith and encourage belief in God's power.
- Exercising spiritual gifts often requires bold faith and action from believers.
- The proper use of spiritual gifts should always be governed by love and aimed at building up others.

Key Themes

- **Diverse Distribution of Gifts:** Each believer is given specific gifts according to the Holy Spirit's discretion, which uniquely equips them to serve the church and glorify God. These gifts range from speaking in tongues to miraculous healings, each serving a specific purpose in God's kingdom.
- **Purpose and Use of Gifts:** Spiritual gifts are not for personal gain but are designed to benefit the entire community of believers. They should be used in humility and love, always pointing back to God and not the individual.
- **Impact of Spiritual Gifts:** The practical outworking of these gifts can lead to significant moments of ministry and transformation, as demonstrated by the healing of a woman in a wheelchair, illustrating the tangible impact of the Holy Spirit's power in modern times.
- **Faith and Action:** The exercise of spiritual gifts often requires an active step of faith, such as encouraging someone to act in faith for healing. This boldness can facilitate miracles and deepen the faith of both the giver and receiver of the gift.
- **Framework of Love:** All spiritual gifts should operate within the framework of love, ensuring they promote peace, edification, and unity within the church. Love is the essential guide that ensures these gifts are used appropriately and effectively.

Conclusion

The Gifts of the Spirit are divine empowerments bestowed upon believers to perform tasks beyond their natural capability for the purpose of building up the church and demonstrating God's sovereign power in the world. These gifts are a testament to the living presence of the Holy Spirit in believers, urging them to seek a deeper relationship with God and to serve His people with humility and love. As the church embraces and utilizes these gifts, it becomes a more effective instrument for God's kingdom, showcasing His love and power to the world.

CHAPTER 4

REPENTANCE

Bible Verse

Acts 3:19-20 (NLT) - "Now repent of your sins and turn to God, so that your sins may be wiped away. Then times of refreshment will come from the presence of the Lord, and he will again send you Jesus, your appointed Messiah."

Introduction

This chapter begins with the author awakening from a vivid and transformative dream about the horrors of hell, prompting a deep reflection on the urgent need for repentance and the profound reality of eternal consequences.

Word of Wisdom

"The enemy is a liar and deceives so many." Jody Keck

Main Theme

The central theme of the chapter emphasizes the critical importance of repentance—a turning away from sin and a turning toward God—as the foundational act that determines one's spiritual trajectory and eternal destiny.

Key Points

- Repentance is essential for cleansing sins and realigning with God's will.
- True repentance involves deep sorrow for sins and a committed turn towards God.
- Hell is depicted vividly to highlight the severe consequences of unrepented sin.
- A dream served as a divine revelation to emphasize the urgency of repentance.
- Eternal destiny is shaped by the choices we make in this life regarding sin and repentance.
- Continuous living in repentance is necessary for a true relationship with God.

Key Themes

- **Divine Revelation Through Dreams:** The author's dream is a stark divine revelation intended to instill the fear of God and highlight the stark realities of hell and the finality of one's choices, serving as a wake-up call to the spiritual complacency many face.
- **Urgency of Repentance:** The chapter underscores repentance as an urgent,

immediate need rather than a distant, optional undertaking. It stresses that delaying repentance can lead to irreversible consequences, as seen through the desperate cries of souls in hell.

- **Hell's Reality:** Descriptions of hell are used not to sensationalize but to confront the reader with the real implications of a life without repentance. This tangible depiction of hell serves to illustrate the eternal separation from God's presence and the unending regret that accompanies it.

- **Impact of Choices on Eternity:** The mirror reflection in the dream symbolizes the self-examination required in repentance, showing that our daily choices and allegiances either align us with God's kingdom or lead us away from it.

- **Lifestyle of Repentance:** Repentance is described not as a one-time event but as a continual process that must characterize the believer's life, involving constant self-awareness, humility, and the pursuit of God's forgiveness and guidance.

Conclusion

The chapter calls for a decisive and immediate response to the message of repentance, urging readers to reflect deeply on their spiritual state and to turn to God without delay. It encourages maintaining a lifestyle of repentance, emphasizing that such a practice is essential for staying aligned with God's will and securing one's eternal destiny in His presence. This act of repentance not only ensures peace with God but also opens the way for ongoing spiritual renewal and personal transformation.

CHAPTER 5

PRAISE AND WORSHIP

Bible Verse

1 Chronicles 16:23-27 (NIV) - "Sing to the Lord, all the earth; proclaim his salvation day after day. Declare his glory among the nations, his marvelous deeds among all peoples. For great is the Lord and most worthy of praise; he is to be feared above all gods. For all the gods of the nations are idols, but the Lord made the heavens. Splendor and majesty are before him; strength and joy are in his dwelling place."

Introduction

The chapter vividly recounts an intense personal and communal experience of praise and worship at the author's home, highlighting the profound connection and divine encounters that can occur through genuine spiritual expressions.

Word of Wisdom

"We praise until the spirit of worship comes. We worship until the glory comes. Then, we stand in the glory." —Ruth Ward Heflin

Main Theme

The narrative explores the dynamic and transformative power of praise and worship, emphasizing how these spiritual practices can foster a deep, personal connection with God, facilitate communal spiritual experiences, and invoke divine presence and intervention.

Key Points

- Praise and worship are essential expressions of our devotion to God.
- Worship can lead to profound spiritual experiences and divine encounters.
- Musical worship is a powerful conduit for expressing our love and reverence for God.
- Communal worship unites believers in a shared experience of God's presence.
- Praise sets the stage for worship, which in turn invites God's glory.
- Worship involves surrender and humility, deepening our relationship with God.

Key Themes

- **Deep Personal Connection Through Worship:** The chapter describes how personal moments of worship can transform into profound spiritual experiences, where the worshippers feel enveloped by God's presence, illustrating the close, intimate relationship one can develop with God through worship.
- **Communal Aspects of Worship:** It highlights the communal power of worship, where individuals, families, and friends gather to share in the spiritual experience, enhancing their collective faith and fostering a stronger community bond in God's presence.
- **Worship as a Gateway to Divine Encounters:** Worship is portrayed not just as an act of religious devotion but as a gateway to encountering the divine, where even angelic presences participate, highlighting the thin veil between the spiritual and the earthly during intense worship.
- **Transformative Power of Musical Worship:** The use of music in worship, including singing in a prayer language and playing instruments like the shofar, acts as a powerful catalyst for spiritual atmospheres, facilitating deeper worship and marking significant spiritual milestones.
- **Praise and Worship as Spiritual Weapons:** The narrative underscores praise and worship as spiritual weapons

that can lead to miraculous outcomes, such as liberation from spiritual and physical confines, much like the biblical story of Paul and Silas.

Conclusion

Praise and worship are depicted as vibrant, essential practices that not only honor God but actively engage His presence, inviting transformative experiences for the individual and the community. These practices are powerful expressions that transcend simple acts of faith, impacting the spiritual realm and bringing about change in the physical world. The chapter calls believers to embrace praise and worship as continuous, integral elements of their spiritual journey, promising a deeper connection with God and a more fulfilled spiritual life.

CHAPTER 6

COMPASSION

Bible Verse

Isaiah 30:18 (NIV) - "Yet the Lord longs to be gracious to you; therefore he will rise up to show you compassion. For the Lord is a God of justice. Blessed are all who wait for him!"

Introduction

This chapter tells the story of a profound encounter between the author and a grieving mother, Andrea, which highlights the deep compassion of God. It captures a moment of divine revelation that brought comfort and transformation through a vision of Andrea's deceased daughter in Heaven.

Word of Wisdom

"All the tears you cry have purpose in Heaven, every single one is collected, and

many are used to wash the feet of the
Master." Jody Keck

Main Theme

The narrative emphasizes the depth of God's
compassion for His children, demonstrated
through our interactions and His attentiveness to
our grief and suffering. It portrays how divine compassion can provide solace and inspire us to act
compassionately towards others.

Key Points

- Compassion is a core attribute of God,
  deeply woven into His interactions
  with us.
- Divine revelations can offer profound
  comfort to those in grief.
- Each tear shed in sorrow is seen and valued
  by God, with a spiritual purpose beyond
  our understanding.
- Personal encounters with God's
  compassion can lead to transformative
  experiences for those involved.
- Compassion compels us to act, moving
  beyond feelings into tangible expressions
  of love and kindness.
- God's compassion is meant to be reflected
  in our actions towards others.

Key Themes

- **Divine Compassion in Personal Grief:** The vision shared with Andrea illustrates that God's compassion extends into the intimate details of our lives, even collecting our tears as treasures that serve a heavenly purpose. This act of divine compassion profoundly affects those who receive such revelations, offering them a new perspective on their suffering.
- **Transformative Power of Compassionate Encounters:** Experiencing God's compassion firsthand not only changes individuals emotionally but also spiritually renews them, prompting shifts in their understanding and relationships with others. These moments are pivotal, turning points that can redefine one's faith and outlook.
- **The Ripple Effect of Compassion:** As demonstrated by the author's interaction with Andrea, one act of compassion can lead to ongoing positive impacts, encouraging those who have been comforted to pass on that compassion. This perpetuates a cycle of kindness and empathy within the community.
- **Compassion as a Reflection of Divine Love:** True compassion is an embodiment of the love and care that God shows us. It calls for us to mirror this divine attribute in our daily interactions, advocating for a lifestyle that actively seeks to alleviate the suffering of others.

- **Compassionate Actions as Spiritual Practice:** Engaging in acts of compassion aligns us with God's will and deepens our spiritual journey. By acting compassionately, we not only aid others but also cultivate our own spiritual growth and closer alignment with God's character.

Conclusion

The chapter concludes by reinforcing the call to live out compassion in our daily lives as a reflection of God's love for us. It encourages readers to engage in acts of kindness and understanding that reach beyond mere feelings, to actively make a difference in the world. By embodying compassion, we not only ease the burdens of others but also bring the kingdom of God closer to reality on earth. Through compassionate actions, we participate in the divine nature and fulfill our call to love as He loves.

CHAPTER 7

FORGIVENESS

Bible Verse

Ephesians 4:31-32 (NIV) - "Get rid of all bitterness, rage and anger, brawling and slander, along with every form of malice. Be kind and compassionate to one another, forgiving each other, just as in Christ God forgave you."

Introduction

This chapter explores the transformative power of forgiveness through a personal story where the author encounters the Holy Spirit's prompt to forgive past wounds, leading to an unexpected reconciliation and profound spiritual freedom.

Word of Wisdom

"Only Jesus can heal the hurt and break the chains of bitterness. He wants to set you free." Jody Keck

. . .

Main Theme

The narrative highlights forgiveness as a divine act that releases us from the chains of bitterness and opens the door to healing and reconciliation, both spiritually and relationally.

Key Points

- Forgiveness is a crucial component of spiritual health and freedom.
- Unresolved bitterness can linger unnoticed until revealed by the Holy Spirit.
- Forgiveness can lead to unexpected and healing encounters.
- True forgiveness views others through the lens of Christ's compassion.
- Forgiveness is not forgetting but choosing not to let the past control the present.
- Surrender to God is essential for genuine forgiveness to occur.

Key Themes

- **Divine Revelation of Unforgiveness:** The Holy Spirit plays a critical role in uncovering hidden unforgiveness, demonstrating that what we may have buried is not always truly resolved. This revelation is often the first step toward healing and spiritual renewal.
- **Healing Through Forgiveness:** The story of forgiving a cousin highlights how

forgiveness can transform personal pain into peace and lead to healing encounters that confirm God's active presence and plan in our lives.

- **Impact of Forgiveness on Relationships:** Forgiveness can drastically change the dynamics of relationships, turning potential lifelong estrangement into opportunities for reconciliation and understanding, as illustrated by the author's unexpected meeting with her cousin.
- **Spiritual and Emotional Liberation:** Forgiveness is depicted as a pathway to spiritual and emotional liberation, freeing individuals from the burdens of past hurts and enabling them to experience joy and peace that were previously hindered by bitterness.
- **Forgiveness as an Ongoing Spiritual Practice:** The chapter emphasizes that forgiveness is not a one-time event but a continuous practice that requires humility, surrender, and a deep reliance on God's strength, fostering an environment where the Holy Spirit can work profoundly within and through us.

Conclusion

The chapter concludes by affirming forgiveness as an essential key to unlocking deeper spiritual experiences and fostering genuine relationships. It calls readers to embrace forgiveness, not only as a response to offenses but as a proactive approach to

living in freedom and grace daily. By practicing forgiveness, we reflect Christ's love and facilitate
God's work of healing and restoration in our lives
and the lives of others.

CHAPTER 8

THE BLOOD OF JESUS

Bible Verse

Revelation 12:11 (NIV) - "They triumphed over him by the blood of the Lamb and by the word of their testimony; they did not love their lives so much as to shrink from death."

Introduction

This chapter unfolds through a vivid dream, emphasizing the protective and victorious power of the blood of Jesus in spiritual warfare. The author recounts a dramatic scene where the blood of Jesus is invoked to conquer demonic forces, symbolizing its ongoing spiritual significance.

Word of Wisdom

"The blood of Jesus covers us and you will not succeed. We are covered by His

blood and you have no authority!"
Jody Keck

Main Theme

The narrative demonstrates the profound spiritual authority and protection afforded by the blood of Jesus, which believers can invoke against evil and in times of danger.

Key Points

- The blood of Jesus is a symbol of ultimate sacrifice and divine protection.
- Invoking the blood of Jesus can provide spiritual victory and safety.
- The power of the blood of Jesus extends beyond physical reality into spiritual battles.
- Believers can use the blood of Jesus as a declaration of faith and authority over darkness.
- The blood of Jesus signifies forgiveness, cleansing, and reconciliation with God.
- Communion is a practice that helps believers remember and honor the sacrifice of Jesus.

Key Themes

- **Spiritual Protection Through the Blood:** The blood of Jesus is not just a historical relic of Christ's sacrifice but serves as a powerful tool for spiritual warfare and protection, as vividly illustrated through the author's dream where demonic forces are vanquished by its invocation.

- **Redemptive Power of the Blood:** The chapter underscores the redemptive power of Jesus' blood, which cleanses sins and restores the believer's relationship with God. This cleansing is both a spiritual purification and a practical empowerment for living free from sin's bondage.
- **Symbolic Representation in Communion:** Communion is highlighted as a sacred act that reconnects believers with the covenant established by Jesus' blood, serving as a constant reminder of His sacrifice and its implications for Christian life.
- **Blood as a Covenantal Seal:** The blood of Jesus is the foundation of a new covenant between God and humanity, replacing old sacrifices with a once-and-for-all offering that assures forgiveness and eternal life for all who believe.
- **Universal Relevance of the Blood:** The power of the blood of Jesus is universally applicable, offering hope and salvation to people from all walks of life, transcending cultural and temporal boundaries to provide a common ground at the foot of the cross.

Conclusion

This chapter concludes by reinforcing the necessity of recognizing and applying the blood of Jesus in the believer's life. It emphasizes that through His blood, believers are equipped to face spiritual challenges with authority and confidence. The narrative encourages an active embrace of this truth, urging readers to live in the freedom and victory that the blood of Jesus secures, thus fulfilling their divine destiny in Christ.

CHAPTER 9

HOLINESS

Bible Verse

Isaiah 6:3-4 (NIV) - "And they were calling to one
another: 'Holy, holy, holy is the Lord Almighty; the
whole earth is full of his glory.' At the sound of
their voices the doorposts and thresholds shook
and the temple was filled with smoke."

Introduction

The chapter begins with a vivid dream where the author experiences a supernatural encounter with God's consuming fire, symbolizing a deep and ongoing process of spiritual purification and the pursuit of holiness.

Word of Wisdom

"I am burning away all chaff."
Jody Keck

Main Theme

The narrative focuses on the concept of holiness as a continuous journey of being set apart for God's purposes, involving spiritual refining and cleansing to align more closely with God's character.

Key Points

- Holiness is about being set apart from sin and dedicated to God's purposes.
- Spiritual encounters can initiate or deepen a commitment to holiness.
- Continuous refinement is a key aspect of living a holy life.
- Holiness involves surrendering all areas of life to God's scrutiny and correction.
- The pursuit of holiness is a response to God's call to be like Him.
- Holiness leads to deeper intimacy and freedom in one's spiritual journey.

Key Themes

- **Dynamic Process of Spiritual Refinement:** The author's personal encounters with God's consuming fire highlight holiness as an active, ongoing process where God burns away impurities to refine and sanctify the believer. This process is not just about removing sin, but about transforming the believer into someone who can carry God's presence more fully.
- **Deepening Intimacy Through Holiness:** As believers engage in this

journey of holiness, they experience deeper levels of intimacy with God. This intimacy is characterized by increased sensitivity to the Holy Spirit's guidance and a greater capacity to experience God's love and power.

- **Holiness as a Response to Divine Love:** The pursuit of holiness is portrayed not as a burdensome duty but as a loving response to God's holiness and His call on our lives. It involves a heartfelt desire to reflect God's purity and love in every aspect of one's being.
- **Practical Implications of Holiness:** Living a holy life involves practical steps such as guarding thoughts, practicing self-control, and being vigilant about influences that can detract from one's spiritual focus. It is about making daily decisions that align with God's will and His Word.
- **Holiness and Spiritual Warfare:** The narrative illustrates that holiness has powerful implications for spiritual warfare, providing believers with authority and protection against evil. The sanctified life is not only about personal purity but also about being equipped to stand against spiritual opposition in strength.

Conclusion

The chapter concludes by encouraging believers to embrace the call to holiness as a joyful, liberating journey that enhances their relationship with God. It asserts that holiness is not achieved through human effort alone but through the empowering presence of the Holy Spirit who enables us to live lives that are pleasing to God. This pursuit of holiness is fundamental to living out the Christian faith, offering peace and power as believers align more closely with the character of Christ.

CHAPTER 10

LOVE

Bible Verse

1 John 4:16 (ESV) - "So we have come to know and to believe the love that God has for us. God is love, and whoever abides in love abides in God, and God abides in him."

Introduction

This chapter narrates a poignant experience where the author shares the burden of grief with a heartbroken mother, reflecting the deep, empathetic nature of God's love and our calling to embody this love in our interactions.

Word of Wisdom

"The grief is too much for them to bear alone. I have entrusted you to share

in their sorrow, to walk alongside them during this time." Jody Keck

Main Theme

The narrative emphasizes love as a profound, selfless commitment to the well-being of others, demonstrated through shared experiences of sorrow and the active choice to comfort and support those in pain.

Key Points

- Love involves deeply empathizing with others' suffering.
- Sharing another's grief is a tangible expression of God's love.
- Love calls us to act beyond mere feelings, taking on others' burdens.
- True love leads to acts of comfort and support.
- Surrendering shared burdens to Jesus brings release and peace.
- Love is exemplified in Jesus and should be mirrored in our lives.

Key Themes

- **Empathetic Sharing of Burdens:** Love sometimes requires us to physically and emotionally share in the burdens of others as a reflection of God's compassion and care. This shared experience not only alleviates the weight on those suffering but also deepens our own understanding of love.

- **Healing through Shared Grief:** By entering into the grief of others and bearing it with them, we participate in a sacred act of healing. This process is transformative for both the giver and the receiver, embodying the healing nature of Christ's love.
- **Divine Purpose in Empathy:** The author's encounter highlights that our empathy has a divine purpose, which is to bring comfort and a sense of solidarity to those experiencing deep sorrow. This purpose aligns with the nature of God, who comforts us in our troubles so that we can comfort others.
- **Love as a Call to Action:** True love compels us to take concrete actions that affirm and support others. These actions often involve personal sacrifice and a willingness to step into uncomfortable or painful situations for the sake of another's well-being.
- **The Transformative Power of Love:** Love has the power to transform both the giver and the receiver, changing lives and healing wounds. It is an active force that God uses to bring about redemption and reconciliation in our broken world.

Conclusion

The chapter concludes by affirming that love is not passive but a dynamic and active force that we are called to express in our daily lives. It challenges readers to embrace love as a way of life, encouraging them to support, comfort, and empathize with others just as Christ does with us. This love is not only a reflection of our faith but also a fundamental expression of who we are called to be as followers of Jesus.

CHAPTER 11

PRAYER

Bible Verse

1 Thessalonians 5:16-18 (NIV) - "Rejoice always,
pray continually, give thanks in all circumstances;
for this is God's will for you in Christ Jesus."

Introduction

This chapter explores the depth and impact of prayer in daily life, illustrating through personal anecdotes how prayer is not only a means of communication with God but also a way to discern and align with His divine will.

Word of Wisdom

"Do you want the blessing or do you want the anointing?" Jody Keck

Main Theme

Prayer is presented as a powerful, dynamic interaction with God that involves more than presenting requests—it is a divine dialogue that guides, transforms, and deepens one's relationship with God.

Key Points

- Prayer is an intimate exchange that affects real-life decisions.
- It involves seeking God's guidance even in everyday decisions like purchasing a car.
- Discernment through prayer can lead to divine revelations and deeper spiritual insights.
- Prayer is not just about asking for things but understanding and aligning with God's will.
- Prayer strengthens our faith and dependence on God.
- Continuous prayer cultivates a deeper relationship with God and a greater sensitivity to His voice.

Key Themes

- **Prayer as a Vehicle for Divine Guidance:** The author's experience with purchasing a car highlights how prayer can be used to seek and receive divine guidance for seemingly mundane decisions. This guidance often comes with a clear choice between mere blessings and deeper spiritual anointing.

- **Transformative Impact of Prayer:** Prayer transforms how believers approach and make decisions, influencing not just the outcomes but also their spiritual growth and understanding of God's priorities. The choice between a blessing and an anointing illustrates how prayer can elevate our decisions from the ordinary to the spiritually significant.
- **Prayer in Response to Life's Challenges:** The author's story of consoling a grieving mother shows how prayer can be a powerful response to life's hardest moments, allowing us to share in and alleviate others' burdens through divine empathy.
- **Discerning and Choosing the Anointing:** The narrative teaches that in prayer, believers are often presented with choices, and discernment is key to choosing paths that are not only good but divinely appointed. This discernment is cultivated through a committed prayer life.
- **Prayer as a Lifestyle:** The author emphasizes that prayer should be continual and ingrained in every aspect of life, not limited to crises or major decisions. This continuous prayer life ensures ongoing communication with God, keeping believers in His will and under His guidance.

Conclusion

The chapter concludes by reinforcing the necessity of making prayer a central part of life. It encourages believers to view prayer not as a sporadic activity but as a constant dialogue with God that informs and transforms every decision. Through prayer, believers can navigate life's challenges with divine wisdom and live out their faith in practical, impactful ways. This ongoing commitment to prayer is essential for maintaining a vibrant, dynamic relationship with God and for fulfilling His purposes in the world.

CHAPTER 12

HUNGER AND ZEAL

Bible Verse

Psalm 107:9 (NIV) - "For he satisfies the thirsty and fills the hungry with good things."

Introduction

This chapter illustrates the transformative power of spiritual hunger and zeal through a personal narrative where the author and her community experience profound encounters with God's presence, leading to miraculous healings and deep spiritual renewal.

Word of Wisdom

"Dive wholeheartedly into knowing God and His purposes. There is so much the Father wants to reveal to you and give you." Jody Keck

Main Theme

The narrative emphasizes that intense spiritual hunger and zeal can lead to extraordinary encounters with God, manifesting His power and presence in tangible, life-changing ways.

Key Points

- Spiritual hunger draws us closer to God, opening doors to His miraculous interventions.
- Zeal for God compels us to engage deeply in spiritual practices and community life.
- True encounters with God often produce visible, powerful results.
- God responds to our spiritual desires by manifesting His presence and power.
- The pursuit of God should be passionate and relentless.
- Spiritual growth is fueled by consistent, fervent prayer and engagement with the Holy Spirit.

Key Themes

- **Transformative Encounters Through Hunger for God:** The author's story of hosting prayer meetings where participants experience God's tangible presence underscores that true spiritual hunger can lead to powerful divine encounters. These moments are not only deeply personal but also communal, impacting all present with a profound sense of God's reality.

- **Zeal as a Catalyst for Miraculous Outcomes:** Zeal for God's presence and will drives the author and her community to see extraordinary healings and spiritual breakthroughs. This intense devotion is shown to be a powerful force that invites God's intervention and fosters a dynamic spiritual environment.
- **Continuous Pursuit of Spiritual Depth:** The author encourages a life of continuous spiritual pursuit, where hunger and zeal are not sporadic but constant traits that drive deeper intimacy with God and consistent spiritual growth.
- **Impact of Spiritual Hunger on Community:** The collective zeal and hunger for God within a community can lead to a revivalistic atmosphere, where many come to faith, are healed, or return to God with renewed passion. This collective dynamic illustrates the contagious nature of genuine spiritual fervor.
- **The Necessity of Balancing Hunger with Discernment:** While hunger draws us to God, discernment guides us in understanding His will. The author's narrative includes moments of decision-making guided by peace and spiritual insight, emphasizing that our zeal must be paired with wisdom to fully align with God's purposes.

Conclusion

The chapter concludes by affirming that hunger and zeal for God are essential for a vibrant spiritual life. These qualities should be nurtured and maintained through regular prayer, worship, and scriptural engagement. By staying spiritually hungry and zealously pursuing God, believers can experience continuous growth, joy, and fulfillment in their spiritual journeys, making significant impacts in their communities and personal lives.

CHAPTER 13

GOODNESS AND KINDNESS

Bible Verse

Luke 6:35 (ESV) - "But love your enemies, and do good, and lend, expecting nothing in return, and your reward will be great, and you will be sons of the Most High, for he is kind to the ungrateful and the evil."

Introduction

This chapter tells a story of personal intervention that embodies the virtues of goodness and kindness, as demonstrated through an encounter with a woman dealing with public shame and personal pain.

Word of Wisdom

"Choose your actions carefully, and always treat others the same way the Master would." Jody Keck

Main Theme

The narrative highlights the transformative power of embodying God's goodness and kindness in real-world situations, using personal testimony to demonstrate how these virtues can change lives.

Key Points

- Goodness and kindness are practical expressions of God's love.
- These virtues can provide significant emotional and spiritual support to those in pain.
- Demonstrating goodness and kindness often involves personal sacrifice.
- Such actions can lead to lasting transformation in others' lives.
- Small gestures, like the giving of stones as symbols of forgiveness and non-judgment, can have profound effects.
- Kindness helps individuals move past difficult chapters in their lives.

Key Themes

- **Transformative Power of Kindness:** The act of sitting beside someone in pain and offering tangible symbols of God's forgiveness can initiate healing and redemption. This illustrates how acts of kindness are not merely gestures but powerful catalysts for change.
- **Symbolic Gestures of Compassion:** The stones given as reminders that no one

is without sin and should not cast stones at others serve as profound tools for forgiveness and self-reflection, symbolizing the weight of judgment and the release it can bring when relinquished.

- **Empathy and Shared Burdens:** Sharing in someone's emotional pain as a deliberate act of kindness underscores the deep connection we can forge when we embody Christ's love and compassion in personal interactions.

- **Long-Term Impact of Kindness:** The lasting impact of a single kind act shows how the seeds of goodness can blossom over time, leading to enduring peace and gratitude in those who have been shown kindness in their darkest moments.

- **Encouragement to Practice Kindness:** The narrative encourages readers to proactively engage in acts of kindness, reinforcing the idea that goodness and kindness should be integral to the Christian life and are within everyone's capacity to give.

Conclusion

The chapter concludes by affirming that goodness and kindness are essential components of Christian character, vital for personal growth and effective ministry. These virtues not only benefit the recipient but also enrich and fulfill the giver, aligning them more closely with God's character. Through stories and teachings, believers are urged to cultivate these traits actively, reflecting Jesus' love in everyday interactions and embracing the profound impact they can have on the world.

CHAPTER 14
KNOWLEDGE

Bible Verse

"Teach me knowledge and good judgement, for I
trust your commands." - Psalm 119:66 NIV

Introduction

Knowledge, we explore the essential role
that divine understanding plays in the
believer's life. Through the personal experience of the author, we witness the transformative impact of applying God's wisdom in
overcoming life's challenges.

Word of Wisdom

*"Understand the weight of your words
and the power of His promises. Embrace
the knowledge of Scripture with the reverence it demands." Jody Keck*

Main Theme

This book delves into the pivotal role knowledge plays in a believer's life, emphasizing the necessity of aligning our actions with God's wisdom to navigate life's complexities successfully.

Key Points

- The lack of scriptural knowledge can lead to unintended negative consequences.
- God's blessings are meant to be received with understanding and gratitude.
- Knowledge of the Word equips believers to handle life's challenges effectively.
- Scriptural wisdom helps in discerning God's will and making sound decisions.
- The importance of continuous learning and growth in faith is emphasized.
- Faith combined with knowledge brings about life-changing breakthroughs.

Key Themes

- **The Power of Words:** The story begins with an innocent yet misguided prayer by Steve, illustrating how a lack of knowledge can lead to devastating outcomes. It emphasizes the need for believers to understand the weight and impact of their words according to scriptural truths.
- **Divine Restoration and Purpose:** Following the loss, the narrative shifts to how God used the situation to teach and mold the author and Steve, showcasing His ability to turn trials into triumphs and

restore what was lost manifold when we align with His divine purpose.

- **The Role of Scripture in Decision Making:** This theme explores how the Bible serves as a guide in making decisions that align with God's will, emphasizing that knowledge of God's Word is fundamental to living a life that pleases Him.
- **The Importance of Spiritual Maturity:** The book underscores the necessity of growing in spiritual maturity through deeper knowledge of God's Word, which equips believers to face various life situations with wisdom and grace.
- **Transformative Impact of Biblical Knowledge:** Through personal testimonies and biblical references, the book illustrates how an understanding of biblical principles can profoundly transform personal lives and influence those around us.

Conclusion

Knowledge serves as a call to deepen our understanding of God's Word. It challenges believers to pursue spiritual growth through continuous learning and application of biblical wisdom. By embodying the principles discussed, readers are encouraged to navigate life's challenges with confidence and live out their divine purpose. This summary not only enlightens but also inspires action, urging each of us to embrace the fullness of life offered through Christ.

CHAPTER 15

PEACE

Bible Verse

Philippians 4:6-7 (NIV) - "Do not be anxious about anything, but in every situation, by prayer and petition, with thanksgiving, present your requests to God. And the peace of God, which transcends all understanding, will guard your hearts and your minds in Christ Jesus."

Introduction

In this chapter, the author narrates an impactful experience during a church service that vividly illustrates the profound peace of God which reaches into the deepest recesses of human suffering and transforms turmoil into tranquility.

Word of Wisdom

"Praise our heavenly Father for His love and tender mercy. Praise Him for His

peace that passes all understanding."
Jody Keck

Main Theme

The central theme explores how the divine peace of God operates beyond human understanding, penetrating deep emotional wounds and bringing restoration and wholeness through the power of the Holy Spirit.

Key Points

- Divine peace is not restricted by our external circumstances.
- God's peace can profoundly transform personal trauma and turmoil.
- True peace involves a direct encounter and intervention from God.
- This peace leads to visible and tangible transformations in individuals.
- God uses personal testimonies and divine revelations to bring healing.
- The peace of God is accessible through prayer and spiritual surrender.

Key Themes

- **Transformation Through Divine Peace:** The peace of God not only soothes but also radically transforms individuals by addressing deep-seated issues that human efforts alone cannot heal. This peace provides both spiritual and emotional liberation.

- **God's Intimate Involvement:** The narrative underscores that God is intimately involved in our lives. He reveals hidden pains and secrets not to shame, but to free us from their bondage, demonstrating that His peace often comes with deep personal revelations and healing.
- **Impact of Divine Revelation:** The personal testimony of the man in the congregation highlights how a divine revelation can authenticate the reality of God's presence and lead to immediate spiritual and emotional healing.
- **The Role of the Holy Spirit:** The Holy Spirit is depicted as the agent through which God's peace is administered, offering not only comfort but also guiding believers into all truth, including uncovering hidden wounds and facilitating healing.
- **The Active Pursuit of Peace:** The chapter illustrates that peace should be actively sought through engagement with the spiritual disciplines of prayer, meditation on the Word, and openness to the Holy Spirit's leading.

Conclusion

The chapter concludes by affirming that peace is a fundamental aspect of the Christian experience, rooted in a deep and personal relationship with God through Jesus Christ. It calls on believers to trust in God's promise to provide peace that surpasses understanding, ensuring that this peace is not merely an abstract concept but a tangible reality that can radically transform lives and circumstances.

CHAPTER 16

OBEDIENCE

Bible Verse

1 Samuel 15:22 (NIV) - "But Samuel replied: 'Does the Lord delight in burnt offerings and sacrifices as much as in obeying the Lord? To obey is better than sacrifice, and to heed is better than the fat of rams.'"

Introduction

In a profound night of prayer, the author shares a vision of financial blessing, setting the stage for a transformative experience of obedience and divine intervention that enriches the participants not just materially but spiritually.

Word of Wisdom

"You never know what one act of obedience will produce." Jody Keck

Main Theme

The theme explores the profound impact of obedience to God's promptings, emphasizing that true obedience is more valuable than sacrifice and can lead to miraculous outcomes.

Key Points

- Obedience to God transcends simple action, tapping into divine promises and provisions.
- The author shared a vision which led to collective obedience among a prayer group.
- Immediate divine responses were observed, manifesting financial blessings for those involved.
- Obedience is linked to faith and the expectation of God's continued goodness.
- Participants experienced significant financial breakthroughs and personal growth.
- The act of obedience extended beyond personal benefit, enabling participants to contribute to God's kingdom.

Key Themes

- **Divine Provision through Obedience:** The unfolding of financial miracles following the group's act of obedience demonstrates how closely God listens and responds when His children act in faith based on His directions.
- **Collective Obedience and Individual Blessing:** The collective action of placing

checkbooks in a basket as a sign of faith shows how communal obedience can lead to individual blessings, reinforcing the concept of community in spiritual acts.

- **Obedience as a Test of Faith:** The initial act of obedience by the author and subsequent follow-through by the group members highlight obedience as both a test and a testament of faith, underscoring its importance in spiritual growth and divine favor.

- **Impact of Obedience on Community:** The shared experience of obedience and its miraculous outcomes fostered a deeper sense of community and shared purpose among the participants, illustrating the broader impacts of obedience beyond individual benefits.

- **Sustained Blessings Through Obedience:** The continuous nature of the blessings received points to the sustained impact of obedience on the lives of believers, suggesting that obedience is not just about single acts but about cultivating a lifestyle that aligns with divine will.

Conclusion

The chapter concludes by affirming the power of obedience as a fundamental spiritual discipline that unlocks divine blessings and transforms lives. It encourages believers to heed the Holy Spirit's promptings, illustrating that obedience is not merely a duty but a gateway to living under God's anointing and provision.

CHAPTER 17

WISDOM

Bible Verse

Proverbs 2:6 (NIV) - "For the Lord gives wisdom; from his mouth come knowledge and understanding."

Introduction

In a poignant narrative, the author shares an experience of praying for a young girl battling cancer, where they received divine wisdom through a dream that profoundly affected the girl's family's journey through her illness.

Word of Wisdom

"Ask Holy Spirit for wisdom and understanding. He wants to use you in miraculous ways to bring peace and comfort to those around you!" Jody Keck

Main Theme

This chapter explores the profound impact of heavenly wisdom received through the Holy Spirit, which helps believers navigate difficult and heart-wrenching situations with divine insight and comfort.

Key Points

- The author receives a transformative dream about a young girl's heavenly peace amidst her struggle with cancer.
- Sharing the dream with the girl's parents brought them comfort and confirmation during a critical decision-making time.
- The dream profoundly impacted the family, helping them prepare for their daughter's peaceful passing.
- Wisdom from God comes through earnest prayer and is crucial in times of need.
- Divine wisdom provides not just knowledge but also comfort and peace to those suffering.
- The experience underscores the importance of seeking and trusting divine guidance in all situations.

Key Themes

- **Receiving and Sharing Divine Wisdom:** The dream about Kendra provided specific, comforting details about her heavenly state, which was crucial in helping her parents cope with her eventual passing. Sharing this wisdom required sensitivity and courage but ultimately brought great solace and spiritual confirmation to the grieving family.

- **Impact of Heavenly Wisdom on Earthly Decisions:** The wisdom received influenced significant decisions regarding Kendra's care, demonstrating how divine insights can guide practical choices and offer peace amidst painful circumstances.
- **Comfort Through Divine Revelations:** The specific details in the dream, particularly the image of Kendra at peace, played a critical role in helping her family deal with their grief, showcasing how God's wisdom often serves to comfort and assure His people.
- **The Role of the Holy Spirit in Imparting Wisdom:** The story highlights the Holy Spirit's role in providing wisdom that is not only timely but also deeply personal and tailored to the needs of His children, reinforcing the belief that God is intimately involved in the lives of believers.
- **Transformation Through Shared Wisdom:** By sharing the dream with Kendra's parents, the author facilitated a spiritual transformation within the family, leading them to a place of peace and acceptance about their daughter's condition, illustrating the powerful impact of acting on divine wisdom.

Conclusion

The chapter concludes by affirming the transformative power of wisdom from God. It encourages believers to actively seek divine wisdom, especially in complex and painful situations, as it not only guides but also comforts and reassures those who are touched by it. Through this story, readers are reminded of the depth of God's love and the profound peace that comes from understanding and accepting His will, even in the most challenging circumstances.

CHAPTER 18

RIGHTEOUSNESS

Bible Verse

Proverbs 21:21 (NIV) - "Whoever pursues righteousness and love finds life, prosperity, and honor."

Introduction

The author shares a powerful encounter with Jesus, who reveals the spiritual burdens His children carry and instructs them to wear His garments of salvation and righteousness instead.

Word of Wisdom

"Step away from the darkness, let the light of His glory shine, and embrace the freedom He offers. Wear your Robe of Righteousness; it's time to remove the veil!" Jody Keck

Main Theme

This chapter delves into the concept of righteousness as a divine attribute that involves shedding worldly burdens and adorning oneself with the spiritual garments of salvation, all through a vivid, personal revelation from Christ.

Key Points

- The author experiences a profound visitation from Jesus, who reveals the spiritual burdens carried by many.
- Jesus instructs to replace these burdens with garments of salvation and righteousness.
- This message was delivered during a women's conference, profoundly impacting many attendees.
- The author emphasizes the universal applicability of this message, extending it to both women and men.
- Righteousness is portrayed not as self-generated but as a divine gift that manifests through our relationship with Christ.

Key Themes

- **The Weight of Spiritual Burdens:** Jesus illustrates the heavy spiritual burdens people wear, such as fear and jealousy, which are likened to a burka that obscures true spiritual freedom. This metaphor highlights the oppressive nature of carrying such weights and the liberation found in Christ.

- **Garments of Salvation and Righteousness:** The narrative extends an invitation to all believers to shed their spiritual burdens and instead clothe themselves with the righteousness given through Christ. This change of garments symbolizes a transformation from sin-bound to grace-filled lives.
- **Impact on the Community:** The author's recounting of this divine revelation at a women's conference catalyzes a profound spiritual awakening among the attendees, demonstrating the power of righteousness to transform lives.
- **Personal Application and Global Message:** The encounter emphasizes that the message of righteousness is not confined to personal transformation but has implications for community healing and global evangelism.
- **Living in True Righteousness:** The chapter encourages readers to embrace a life of righteousness that goes beyond superficial piety and deeply influences one's character, choices, and conduct, reflecting the nature of Jesus.

Conclusion

The chapter concludes by reinforcing the importance of embracing and living out righteousness in everyday life. It calls on readers to recognize their spiritual burdens, accept the righteousness imparted by Christ, and manifest this gift through actions that reflect God's love and justice. This journey of righteousness is not only about personal sanctification but also about becoming beacons of God's transformative power in the world.

CHAPTER 19

HUMILITY

Bible Verse

Matthew 18:4 (KJV) - "Whosoever therefore shall humble himself as this little child, the same is greatest in the kingdom of heaven."

Introduction

During a peaceful morning devotion, the author experiences a profound moment of humility and worship, which she shares with her granddaughter, leading to a deeper understanding and appreciation of God's presence.

Word of Wisdom

"I often tell people one of the best ways to describe when He draws so near is that it just feels like liquid love is being poured over you." Jody Keck

Main Theme

This chapter explores the essence of humility, demonstrating it through a personal story of worship and surrender, highlighting the transformative power of embracing humility before God.

Key Points

- The author begins her day with a quiet time outdoors, feeling a strong connection to God's creation.
- She experiences a profound moment of humility and worship, prostrating before God as His presence fills the room.
- Her granddaughter joins her in worship, showing the impact of humility across generations.
- They spend the day together, discussing the significance of their spiritual experience.
- The author reflects on the beauty of creation and the blessings of a humble heart.

Key Themes

- **Experiencing God's Presence:** The author's encounter with God's overwhelming presence underscores the closeness that humility fosters between the believer and the divine, illustrating how such moments can deeply impact one's spiritual life.
- **Generational Influence of Humility:** The spontaneous act of worship by the

granddaughter highlights the powerful, generational impact of demonstrating humility, suggesting that such qualities can inspire and nurture similar responses in others, especially young children.

- **Spiritual Teachings on Humility:** The narrative weaves in teachings about humility, using the personal story as a backdrop to explore deeper spiritual truths about surrendering to God's will and experiencing His grace.

- **The Role of Nature in Spiritual Experience:** The author's appreciation for nature is woven into her experience of humility, suggesting that the beauty of the natural world can enhance one's perception of God's majesty and foster a humble heart.

- **Transformation Through Humility:** The chapter emphasizes that true humility can lead to profound personal and spiritual transformation, enriching one's relationship with God and enhancing one's ability to impact others positively.

Conclusion

This chapter concludes by encouraging readers to seek humility in their daily lives as a means to experience God's presence more fully. It calls on the reader to embrace the simplicity and purity of a humble heart, which aligns with Christ's teachings and leads to a life rich with God's peace and joy.

CHAPTER 20

AUTHORITY

Bible Verse

Revelation 2:26 (NIV) - "To the one who is victorious and does my will to the end, I will give authority over the nations."

Introduction

While on vacation in Sedona, the author encounters spiritual warfare in a shop, which underscores the Christian's spiritual authority to overcome darkness through Christ.

Word of Wisdom

"He tells us in Luke 10:19, 'Behold, I have given you authority to tread upon serpents and scorpions, and over all the power of the enemy: and nothing shall in any wise hurt you.'"

. . .

Main Theme

This chapter delves into the concept of spiritual authority, illustrating how believers are empowered by God to confront and overcome spiritual darkness in everyday encounters.

Key Points

- The author and her sister experience God's creation in Sedona but encounter spiritual darkness in local shops.
- A shop attendant reacts fearfully to the author's presence due to a demonic influence.
- After leaving the shop, the author feels compelled to return and minister to the attendant, demonstrating the exercise of spiritual authority.
- The shop attendant locks the door, preventing any interaction, but the author continues to pray outside.
- The encounter emphasizes the real and present battles between spiritual forces that believers are called to engage with.

Key Themes

- **Spiritual Authority Over Darkness:** The chapter vividly illustrates the Christian's authority over demonic forces, emphasizing that believers are equipped to face and overcome spiritual opposition through the power vested in them by Christ.

- **Responsibility of Believers:** It highlights the believer's responsibility to actively use their God-given authority to bring light into dark places, reflecting Jesus' mandate to set captives free.
- **Encountering Spiritual Warfare:** The unexpected spiritual warfare encountered in a mundane setting teaches that spiritual battles can arise anywhere, and Christians must be prepared to respond with authority and prayer.
- **Impact of Prayer and Presence:** The author's decision to pray for the shop attendant from outside the locked shop underscores the power of prayer and the Holy Spirit's presence to transcend physical barriers in spiritual warfare.
- **Discernment in Spiritual Encounters:** The chapter calls for discernment in recognizing spiritual battles in daily life and understanding when and how to exercise spiritual authority effectively.

Conclusion

The chapter concludes by encouraging believers to embrace and exercise their spiritual authority with confidence and humility, trusting in God's power to work through them to accomplish His purposes on earth. It inspires readers to be vigilant and proactive in spiritual warfare, using their authority to bring God's light and freedom to those oppressed by darkness.

CHAPTER 21

UNITY

Bible Verse

1 Corinthians 1:10 NIV - "I appeal to you, brothers and sisters, in the name of our Lord Jesus Christ, that all of you agree with one another in what you say and that there be no divisions among you, but that you be perfectly united in mind and thought."

Introduction

During a peaceful Sabbath, the author experiences a revelation from the Holy Spirit about unity, symbolized by a tapestry that represents the interconnected lives and destinies of believers.

Word of Wisdom

"You don't see the finished picture, but I do. Trust me." - This reminds us that God sees the complete and beautiful

outcome of our interconnected lives, urging us to trust in His divine arrangement.
Jody Keck

Main Theme

This chapter explores the concept of unity within the Christian faith, emphasizing how believers are intricately woven together like a tapestry, each playing a unique and essential role in God's divine plan.

Key Points

- Unity is portrayed as a divine tapestry with each believer being an integral thread.
- The author receives a revelation about unity during a moment of relaxation and contemplation.
- The Holy Spirit uses the tapestry metaphor to illustrate the complex yet beautiful interplay of individual lives.
- This unity transcends individual understanding, requiring faith and trust in God's perfect design.
- The narrative encourages embracing unity to reflect God's comprehensive and meticulous plan for humanity.

Key Themes

- **Divine Tapestry of Lives:** The tapestry metaphor beautifully illustrates how individual threads (believers) contribute to a larger, cohesive picture, symbolizing unity in diversity within the church.

- **Trust in God's Vision:** Just as the back of a tapestry contains knots and tangled threads, life's challenges are part of a bigger plan that God orchestrates, which requires our trust and faith in His ultimate wisdom.
- **Unity as God's Design:** Unity is shown not as a human contrivance but as a divine orchestration where each believer plays a crucial role, akin to threads in a tapestry, contributing to the overall unity and purpose of God's kingdom.
- **Spiritual Reflection and Action:** The chapter calls for personal reflection on the part of believers to understand their role in God's plan, urging them to act in ways that promote unity and collective growth within the church.
- **Practical Implications of Unity:** Emphasizes the need for believers to live out unity in practical ways, encouraging mutual support, shared goals, and a communal approach to faith that mirrors the unity of the Father, Son, and Holy Spirit.

Conclusion

The chapter concludes by reiterating the power and necessity of unity among believers, encouraging them to view their contributions through the lens of a larger divine tapestry. It is a call to live in harmony, embodying the unity that Jesus prayed for, which stands as a testament to the world of God's love and transformative power.

CHAPTER 22

DELIVERANCE

Bible Verse

Ephesians 6:12 NIV - "For our struggle is not against flesh and blood, but against the rulers, against the authorities, against the powers of this dark world and against the spiritual forces of evil in the heavenly realms."

Introduction

One serene evening, a knock at the door led to a profound experience of spiritual warfare and deliverance, showcasing God's power to free us from the grips of darkness.

Word of Wisdom

"No matter what you are battling, remember that He who is in you is greater than he who is in the world." - This statement underscores the Christian's

authority over demonic powers through Christ.

Main Theme

This chapter narrates a gripping account of spiritual deliverance, detailing an encounter where the author assists a troubled individual, Mindy, in overcoming demonic oppression through the power of prayer and the authority given by Christ.

Key Points

- Mindy visited seeking help, revealing her struggles with life choices and demonic oppression.
- The encounter escalated to a spiritual battle involving visible manifestations of demonic presence.
- The author engaged in intense prayer and deliverance, leading to Mindy's freedom.
- The experience reaffirmed the power and authority Christians hold over demonic forces.
- Mindy's transformation highlighted the transformative power of deliverance and the grace of God.

Key Themes

- **Spiritual Warfare Visibility:** The physical and spiritual manifestations during the deliverance process emphasize the reality and intensity of spiritual warfare Christians may face.

- **Authority over Demons:** The story illustrates the biblical truth that believers are endowed with authority to cast out demons and wage spiritual warfare effectively.
- **Transformation through Deliverance:** Mindy's deliverance wasn't just about casting out demons; it also involved healing and profound spiritual renewal, showcasing deliverance as a gateway to a restored life.
- **The Role of Faith in Deliverance:** The author's unshakeable faith and the spiritual authority exercised during the deliverance underscore the critical role of faith in overcoming demonic influences.
- **Continued Prayer and Vigilance:** Post-deliverance, the narrative stresses the importance of continued prayer and spiritual vigilance to maintain the freedom won through Christ.

Conclusion

The chapter concludes by encouraging believers to embrace their divine authority to seek deliverance from spiritual bondage. It calls for a deeper engagement with the spiritual tools provided through faith in Christ, ensuring believers can effectively confront and overcome the forces of darkness in their lives.

CHAPTER 23

SURRENDER

Bible Verse

Galatians 2:20 NIV - "I have been crucified with Christ and I no longer live, but Christ lives in me. The life I now live in the body, I live by faith in the Son of God, who loved me and gave himself for me."

Introduction

In a night of deep spiritual engagement, the author experiences a profound encounter, receiving a message that emphasizes the importance of complete surrender to God's plan.

Word of Wisdom

"Surrender is not about losing; it is about winning God's ultimate purpose for our lives." Jody Keck

Main Theme

This chapter delves into the transformative power of surrendering to God's will, illustrating how yielding fully to God's divine plan can lead to remarkable spiritual insights and alignment with heavenly purposes.

Key Points

- Surrender involves relinquishing control to God and trusting His guidance fully.
- The author receives a mysterious spiritual message during a night of prayer.
- This message later connects to a prophetic dream received by another believer, emphasizing the global impact of spiritual surrender.
- The narrative unfolds to reveal the author's role in a larger divine story tied to revival and end-time harvest.
- The profound personal and communal transformations that follow highlight the power of true spiritual surrender.

Key Themes

- **The Connection Between Surrender and Divine Purpose:** Surrendering to God allows individuals to become part of a larger story, where personal transformation aligns with God's overarching plans for revival and healing.
- **The Power of Prophetic Insight in Surrender:** The author's experience illustrates how surrender can open the

door to receiving profound prophetic insights that clarify and guide God's people towards their divine destinies.

- **Impact of Surrender on Personal and Community Growth:** The narrative shows that surrender not only transforms individuals but also has the potential to impact communities and generations, linking current believers with historical and future movements of God.
- **Surrender as a Pathway to Spiritual Authority:** Through surrender, believers are imbued with spiritual authority to carry forward God's work, as illustrated by the author's connection to significant prophetic figures and movements.
- **The Role of Surrender in Fulfilling God's Promises:** The chapter emphasizes that surrender is crucial for the fulfillment of God's promises, as it allows believers to step into roles that God has ordained for them, impacting the church and the world.

Conclusion

The chapter concludes by encouraging readers to embrace surrender as a key spiritual discipline that unlocks God's promises and power. It calls on believers to yield completely to God's will, thereby activating their part in His divine plan and experiencing the fullness of His presence and purpose.

CHAPTER 24

BAPTISM OF THE HOLY SPIRIT

Bible Verse

Acts 2:1-4 NIV - "When the day of Pentecost came, they were all together in one place. Suddenly a sound like the blowing of a violent wind came from heaven and filled the whole house where they were sitting. They saw what seemed to be tongues of fire that separated and came to rest on each of them. All of them were filled with the Holy Spirit and began to speak in other tongues as the Spirit enabled them."

Introduction

The author recounts a personal transformative experience of the baptism of the Holy Spirit, beginning with a desire for a deeper relationship with God, culminating in a powerful spiritual encounter during worship that altered her spiritual trajectory.

Word of Wisdom

"When we fully surrender, the Holy Spirit moves mightily, baptizing us with fire and a passion for Christ that transcends human understanding." Jody Keck

Main Theme

This chapter explores the profound and life-changing experience of the baptism of the Holy Spirit, which empowers believers with divine gifts and ignites a deeper communion with God.

Key Points

- The author sought deeper spiritual truths beyond traditional teachings, driven by a desire to experience God's miraculous power.
- A pivotal moment of spiritual encounter is described during a church service, where the author experiences the physical manifestation of Jesus and the Holy Spirit.
- Speaking in tongues marked the personal baptism of the Holy Spirit for the author, enhancing her spiritual gifts and understanding.
- This baptism catalyzed a new boldness in ministry and a heightened intimacy in her relationship with God.

The chapter emphasizes the transformation that follows the baptism of the Holy Spirit, affecting all areas of a believer's life.

Key Themes

- **Spiritual Hunger Leads to Divine Encounters:** The author's journey underscores the importance of spiritual hunger and openness to God's power, which prepares the heart for the baptism of the Holy Spirit.
- **The Transformative Power of the Holy Spirit:** Experiencing the baptism of the Holy Spirit brings about a profound transformation, equipping believers with spiritual gifts and a newfound boldness in their faith walk.
- **Enhanced Relationship with God:** The baptism of the Holy Spirit deepens one's relationship with God, enabling a more intimate prayer life and understanding of the scriptures.
- **Empowerment for Service:** Beyond personal transformation, the baptism equips believers for service, enabling them to operate in gifts of prophecy, healing, and speaking in tongues, thereby contributing to the body of Christ.
- **Continual Impact of the Holy Spirit's Baptism:** The chapter highlights the ongoing impact of the Holy Spirit's baptism in a believer's life, fostering continuous growth, empowerment, and effectiveness in ministry.

Conclusion

The baptism of the Holy Spirit is presented as an essential and transformative experience for every believer, empowering them with divine gifts and aligning them closer to God's purpose. It is a pivotal event that enhances one's spiritual journey, enabling them to live out a faith that is dynamic, powerful, and effective in witnessing to the world.

CHAPTER 25

DISCERNMENT

Bible Verse

1 John 4:1 ESV - "Beloved, do not believe every spirit, but test the spirits to see whether they are from God, for many false prophets have gone out into the world."

Introduction

This chapter reveals the importance and transformative nature of spiritual discernment, highlighting real-life experiences that showcase how divine insight can guide believers in both profound and practical ways. Through attentiveness to the Holy Spirit's guidance, the author demonstrates how discernment helps to bring clarity, assurance, and alignment with God's will.

Word of Wisdom

"Discernment allows us to see beyond the immediate and into the truth that

God reveals, grounding us in faith and guiding our steps." Jody Keck

Main Theme

The chapter emphasizes discernment as a divine gift that enables believers to navigate spiritual realities, make wise decisions, and remain steadfast in truth, serving as a spiritual compass grounded in the Holy Spirit's guidance.

Key Points

- Discernment is a spiritual ability to distinguish truth from deception, rooted in a relationship with the Holy Spirit.
- Real-life experiences illustrate how discernment can reveal God's intentions and empower believers to respond faithfully.
- Growth in discernment requires time spent in communion with Jesus, allowing His Spirit to reveal deeper truths.
- Discernment involves recognizing the difference between God's voice and the subtle deceptions of the enemy.
- John 16:13 highlights the Holy Spirit as our guide into all truth, affirming the divine source of discernment.
- Discernment equips believers to identify and withstand false teachings and influences, guarding their faith.

Key Themes

- **Divine Insight in Everyday Life:** Discernment goes beyond spiritual understanding to include real-life applications, revealing God's will in seemingly ordinary situations and helping believers make choices aligned with His plans.
- **Testing Spirits and Avoiding Deception:** Scripture calls us to "test the spirits" (1 John 4:1), enabling believers to distinguish between divine guidance and spiritual deception, a vital safeguard in a world filled with mixed messages.
- **The Holy Spirit as the Ultimate Source:** Discernment is empowered by the Holy Spirit, who grants insight and wisdom; through Him, believers gain clarity and assurance in spiritual matters and earthly decisions alike.
- **Recognizing and Resisting the Enemy:** Discernment enables believers to identify and stand against the tactics of the enemy, ensuring that faith remains unshaken in the face of adversity or falsehood.
- **Discernment as a Spiritual Compass:** Discernment serves as a spiritual compass, guiding believers toward eternal values over worldly temptations and helping them pursue a life in alignment with Kingdom purposes.

Conclusion

Discernment is an invaluable gift that deepens our relationship with God, helping us to navigate life's complexities with wisdom and integrity. Through discernment, believers can see beyond immediate circumstances, stand firm in the truth, and partner with the Holy Spirit to reveal God's glory on earth. This spiritual insight is key to living a life that embodies and reflects the wisdom, grace, and truth of the Kingdom.

CHAPTER 26

HONOR

Bible Verse

Romans 12:10 NIV - "Be devoted to one another in love. Honor one another above yourselves."

Introduction

This chapter explores the spiritual depth of honoring others as a divine act of love and respect. Through personal stories and scripture, it emphasizes that honoring others is not only an expression of humility but a profound way to embody God's love and presence in our lives.

Word of Wisdom

"Honor flows from a heart of humility and reflects the immeasurable love of God, enriching both the giver and the receiver."
Jody Keck

Main Theme

The heart of honor lies in acknowledging the intrinsic value of each person as a creation of God. Honoring others builds unity, fosters humility, and is a reflection of the divine love and respect we are called to emulate in our relationship with Christ and each other.

Key Points

- Honor begins with a heart of love and respect for others as valuable creations of God.
- Christ's example teaches us to honor all people, regardless of status or background, as an act of worship to God.
- Honor should extend to every aspect of life, including our families, communities, leaders, and faith commitments.
- Small acts of honor, such as respecting others in speech and actions, contribute to a stronger foundation of humility and unity.
- Honoring others ultimately brings glory to God, aligning our actions with His divine love.
- Cultivating honor in relationships can transform them, fostering peace and closeness as we reflect Christ's love.

Key Themes

- **Honoring God and Jesus:** Our first priority is to honor God, with whom all true honor begins. Honoring Jesus as we honor the Father reflects our reverence and gratitude for the sacrifice He made for us.

- **Respecting All People:** True honor sees beyond outward appearances, recognizing the intrinsic worth God places in each person. When we approach others with compassion, we align ourselves with God's love and vision for humanity.
- **Honor Within Relationships:** Acts of love and service within families, marriages, and friendships strengthen these bonds, reflecting the selfless love Christ exemplifies. Honoring others in close relationships is an opportunity to demonstrate God's love tangibly.
- **Honor Through Obedience and Forgiveness:** Honoring others includes respecting authority, forgiving generously, and living with integrity. By respecting our commitments and showing mercy, we embody God's grace and make His love visible to the world.
- **Honor as a Lifestyle:** Honor can be woven into daily life through kindness, generosity, and authenticity. Small, sincere actions of respect create an atmosphere of peace and love, showcasing the glory of God to those around us.

Conclusion

Honor is a divine key that opens doors to deeper relationships and richer expressions of God's love.

By living in humility and compassion, we honor others and reflect the heart of Christ. Embracing honor in all aspects of life allows God's presence to shine through us, creating a legacy of love, respect, and unity that blesses everyone we encounter.

CHAPTER 27

GENEROSITY

Bible Verse

Psalms 112:5 NIV - "Good will come to those who are generous and lend freely, who conduct their affairs with justice."

Introduction

This chapter explores the profound impact of generosity, showing that even the smallest acts of giving can yield an immeasurable harvest over time. Through personal experiences and reflections on scripture, we are reminded that God values every act of kindness and blesses us abundantly as we give freely and with a heart aligned to His love.

Word of Wisdom

"When we are generous, we are mirroring His love in action, reflecting the One who gave everything for us." Jody Keck

Main Theme

Generosity is a powerful expression of God's love. It aligns our lives with His heart, reminding us that every blessing we have is ultimately His and should be used to impact others and expand His Kingdom.

Key Points

- Generosity is a reflection of God's boundless love and the ultimate sacrifice of His Son.
- Every act of giving, whether big or small, leaves a lasting impact, creating a ripple effect that can change lives.
- God rewards faith-filled giving, as illustrated in countless scriptures, including Hebrews 6:10.
- True generosity involves more than financial giving—it includes sharing time, talents, and spiritual gifts.
- Acts of generosity can often be the answer to someone else's prayer, allowing God's love to flow through us.
- Generosity deepens our faith by reminding us to trust God as the provider of all we have and need.

Key Themes

- **Generosity as Worship:** Every act of giving is a form of worship and trust in God. When we offer our resources and time to others, we acknowledge that all good things are from God and return to Him as acts of devotion.

- **Kingdom Impact of Small Acts:** Even modest acts of generosity, like the widow's offering, can yield significant spiritual outcomes. Jesus highlighted her offering as an example of sacrificial giving, underscoring that small gestures can have far-reaching effects when given in faith.
- **Faith and Generosity:** Being generous stretches our faith, teaching us reliance on God as we share our blessings with others. This heart posture cultivates a spirit of gratitude, encouraging us to hold our possessions loosely and trust God for our needs.
- **The Spiritual Legacy of Giving:** Generosity isn't just about helping others; it's about building a legacy that glorifies God. Each act of giving has the potential to impact lives for generations, just as seeds grow into great trees over time.
- **Becoming a Vessel of Blessing:** Generosity enables us to partner with the Holy Spirit, becoming channels of God's love and provision. By giving freely, we align ourselves with the mission of spreading God's love and mercy to a world in need.

Conclusion

Generosity is a profound invitation to participate in God's love, mirroring His character and blessing others. Each act of giving is a key that unlocks more of God's presence in our lives, expanding His Kingdom and deepening our relationship with Him. Embracing generosity, we become vessels of

His grace, illuminating His goodness in our world. Let this be a lifelong practice, knowing that every gift offered in faith brings joy to God's heart and light to others.

CHAPTER 28

DECLARATIONS

Bible Verse

Proverbs 18:21 NIV - "The tongue has the power of life and death, and those who love it will eat its fruit."

Introduction

This chapter focuses on the power of spoken words and their profound spiritual impact. Through declarations aligned with God's Word, believers can activate His promises, break strongholds, and invite transformative power into their lives. The importance of guarding our speech and intentionally speaking words of life is underscored as a means of drawing nearer to God's will.

Word of Wisdom

"Our confession will either imprison us or set us free. Our confession is the result

of our believing, and our believing is the result of our right or wrong thinking." — Kenneth Hagin

Main Theme

Declarations, when aligned with God's truth, wield spiritual power to shape our lives, influence others, and create atmospheres for God's presence. By speaking life and faith, we actively participate in God's work, unleashing His supernatural power and promises.

Key Points

- Words have the power to create or destroy, bringing either life or death into our lives and situations.
- Declarations rooted in God's truth are a spiritual tool to break chains and shift circumstances.
- Consistent, faith-filled declarations align us with God's promises and invite His influence.
- Speaking truth and life reflects the condition of our hearts, as Jesus taught in Matthew 12:34.
- The armor of God, particularly the "sword of the Spirit," symbolizes our authority to declare God's Word in spiritual warfare.
- Confessions and declarations of faith help maintain a mindset of victory, trust, and divine perspective.

Key Themes

- **Power of Words as Creative Force:** God created the world through spoken words, illustrating the creative potential in declarations. Our words, aligned with His truth, have the power to shape realities and open doors to His Kingdom on earth.
- **Speaking Life or Death:** Proverbs 18:21 reminds us that our words hold spiritual weight, capable of releasing blessings or curses. When we choose life-giving speech, we partner with God in bringing His love and light into our lives and relationships.
- **Reflection of the Heart:** Jesus taught that our words reflect our inner condition. Speaking words of faith, love, and hope aligns our hearts with God's character, shaping a life that bears witness to His goodness.
- **Declarations as Weapons in Spiritual Warfare:** The Word of God is a powerful defense in battles against spiritual opposition. By declaring God's truth over our lives, we wield the "sword of the Spirit," actively countering lies and discouragement from the enemy.
- **Confessions that Align with God's Promises:** Declarations of hope, healing, and provision position us to receive the fullness of God's blessings. Our words can pave the way for divine encounters and miraculous breakthroughs, as we declare His promises with expectation.

Conclusion

Declarations are a key to a powerful and faith-filled life. As we intentionally speak God's truth, we align ourselves with His will and become vessels of His transformative power. Let your words be filled with life, faith, and His promises, knowing they connect you to the heart of the Father. Embrace the power of declarations, releasing faith, hope, and truth into your world, and witness the supernatural as God's Kingdom is manifested through the words you speak.

CHAPTER 29

STEWARDSHIP

Bible Verse

Proverbs 3:9 NIV - "Honor the Lord with your wealth, with the firstfruits of your crops; then your barns will be filled to overflowing, and your vats will brim over with new wine."

Introduction

This chapter explores the profound responsibility and blessing of stewardship. As stewards, we are entrusted by God to manage His blessings—our resources, time, and talents—for His glory. Through faithful stewardship, we experience His provision, and with a heart of gratitude, we grow in trust, generosity, and obedience to His will.

Word of Wisdom

"God has not called me to be successful. He called me to be faithful." —Mother Teresa

. . .

Main Theme

Stewardship is about more than just managing resources; it's about recognizing God as the source of all blessings and using what He gives to honor Him. Faithful stewardship leads to divine multiplication and opens doors for unexpected blessings.

Key Points

- Stewardship acknowledges that everything we have comes from God and is meant for His purposes.
- Giving generously is a reflection of faith and positions us to experience God's abundant provision.
- Stewardship requires integrity and intentionality with our resources, time, and talents.
- Our time is an offering to God and should be used in ways that bring glory to Him.
- Financial stewardship is a declaration of trust in God's provision, inviting His blessings.
- Stewardship of talents allows God's anointing to flow through us, impacting others.

Key Themes

- **God as the Source of All Blessings:** Stewardship begins with understanding that all we possess, from our finances to our skills, is a gift from God. This awareness fosters gratitude and drives us to use His blessings responsibly.

- **Generosity as Faith in Action:** Giving is an act of faith that honors God and enables His work to multiply. By sowing into others and the Kingdom, we open ourselves to the abundance He has prepared.
- **Integrity in Financial Stewardship:** Financial stewardship is not only about managing funds wisely but also about being accountable with what we receive. Honoring God with our wealth invites His presence into our financial matters.
- **Time as a Divine Resource:** Time is a precious and limited resource. How we spend it reflects our priorities, and when we offer it back to God, we draw closer to Him and impact others in meaningful ways.
- **Using Talents for God's Glory:** Our talents are channels for God's anointing. When we steward them well, they become tools for ministry, inspiring and blessing others and revealing God's love and power.

Conclusion

Stewardship is a calling to faithfully manage the blessings God has given us. As we align our resources, time, and talents with His purposes, we position ourselves for deeper spiritual growth and divine provision. Stewarding what God has entrusted to us is a daily commitment that brings glory to Him and impacts the lives of others. Choose wisely how you spend what God has given, and let each act of stewardship reflect your devotion and gratitude to Him.

BELIEF

Bible Verse

Mark 11:24 NIV - "Therefore I tell you, whatever you ask for in prayer, believe that you have received it, and it will be yours."

Introduction

Belief forms the foundation of our faith, extending beyond simple hope to confident expectation in the living, active God. Through belief, we move from merely asking in prayer to receiving with assurance, trusting that God's promises hold true and that His presence is working powerfully in our lives.

Word of Wisdom

"He does not believe who does not live according to his belief." —Thomas Fuller

Main Theme

Belief is more than just asking; it's an active stance of faith that brings life and confidence into our relationship with God. This chapter explores the dynamic shift from asking to believing, illustrating how living faith transforms prayer, draws us closer to God, and aligns our hearts with His will.

Key Points

- True belief moves us from simply asking to confidently receiving what God has promised.
- Belief in God is central to our relationship with Him, forming the basis of our faith.
- Faith is strengthened by understanding that God is living, present, and active.
- Believing deeply leads to a firm, unshakable confidence in God's plans and power.
- Faith-filled belief enables us to view circumstances from a Kingdom perspective.
- Trust in God's promises transforms our perspective, making breakthroughs and miracles possible.

Key Themes

- **Belief as the Foundation of Faith:**
  Belief is more than historical understanding; it's knowing that God is alive and active in our lives today. True belief opens our hearts to a dynamic,

personal relationship with Him and strengthens our trust in His plans.

- **Belief in the Power of Prayer:** Moving from asking to believing reshapes how we approach prayer, infusing it with confidence and expectation. When we believe, we claim the promises of God as already accomplished, transforming our lives and drawing us into deeper reliance on Him.
- **The Transformative Nature of Faith:** Faith based on belief empowers us to view every situation through the lens of God's greater plan. As we cultivate belief, our challenges shift from obstacles to opportunities for God to reveal His power.
- **Authority in Christ through Belief:** Knowing who we are in Christ, we believe and walk in the authority He has given us. This faith builds courage and boldness to declare God's truths, live out our purpose, and influence the world around us.
- **Belief in God's Word:** Faith in His Word underpins the promises that fuel our hope and anticipation. By believing in His promises, we find strength, healing, and transformation, trusting that nothing is impossible in His Kingdom.

Conclusion

Belief is a vital key in living a life filled with God's presence, power, and promises. As we grow in belief, we step into a deeper walk of faith, partnering with God's will and opening ourselves to receive all

He has prepared for us. Let belief guide you into a life of supernatural expectation and bold prayer, reflecting His Kingdom on earth.

CHAPTER 31

GENTLENESS

Bible Verse

Ephesians 4:2 NIV - "Be completely humble and gentle; be patient, bearing with one another in love."

Introduction

Gentleness is a powerful blend of strength and compassion, a quality reflecting God's tender care for each of us. This chapter explores how God calls us to gentleness in both spirit and action, empowering us to bring healing, grace, and kindness to others while navigating life's storms with a peaceful heart.

Word of Wisdom

"Nothing is so strong as gentleness, nothing so gentle as real strength." —
Francis de Sales

. . .

Main Theme

Gentleness is not about weakness; it's a profound strength that flows from humility, patience, and love, modeled by Jesus. When we embody gentleness, we are equipped to share in others' burdens and extend God's compassion and healing through our actions.

Key Points

- Gentleness is a strength rooted in God's peace, guiding us in kindness and humility.
- Christ's life exemplifies gentleness as a powerful force of love and compassion.
- A gentle spirit fosters patience and understanding toward others' struggles.
- Gentleness is listed as a fruit of the Spirit, underscoring its importance in Christian character.
- We are called to approach others' pain with a soft heart, offering hope and encouragement.
- Being gentle in our actions reflects the love of Jesus, allowing His healing to flow through us.

Key Themes

- **Gentleness as Inner Strength:** True gentleness arises from inner peace and strength, allowing us to face adversity calmly. This strength enables us to support others without judgment, offering empathy and understanding.

- **The Gentle Nature of Jesus:** Jesus exemplified gentleness, especially in His interactions with the brokenhearted. His compassionate approach to healing and guiding others demonstrates a love that is deeply kind and unconditionally forgiving.
- **Bearing Others' Burdens in Gentleness:** Gentleness equips us to come alongside those in need, sharing in their struggles and encouraging them with patience and wisdom. This selfless support mirrors the gentle heart of the Father.
- **Gentleness as a Fruit of the Spirit:** The Bible emphasizes gentleness as a fruit of the Spirit, signifying its role in Christian life and growth. By fostering this quality, we allow the Holy Spirit to work through us, shaping us into reflections of Christ's love.
- **Gentleness in Wisdom and Guidance:** When offering counsel, gentleness allows us to impart wisdom without harshness, creating an environment of trust and openness. A gentle approach invites others to receive guidance with a willing heart, knowing it is rooted in love.

Conclusion

Embracing gentleness enables us to display Christ's love in a world in need of kindness, patience, and grace. It is a powerful key that reflects God's compassion, offering peace to others and glorifying Him. Let gentleness shape your interactions, bearing others' burdens with a loving spirit and inviting His healing presence into every encounter.

CHAPTER 32

COURAGE

Bible Verse

Deuteronomy 31:6 NIV - "Be strong and courageous. Do not be afraid or terrified because of them, for the Lord your God goes with you; he will never leave you nor forsake you."

Introduction

In times of fear and uncertainty, courage is a call to rely on God's strength within us to face challenges with unwavering faith. True courage comes from a deep trust in God's promises, understanding that He is with us in every battle. This chapter reveals that God's angel armies fight alongside us, reminding us that we are not alone in our struggles.

Word of Wisdom

"Courage is what it takes to stand up and speak; courage is also what it takes

to sit down and listen." —Winston Churchill

Main Theme

Courage is rooted in trust in God's omnipotence and His promises to protect and guide us. It's not just a physical display of strength but a profound spiritual resilience to step forward in faith despite fear, strengthened by the Holy Spirit's presence.

Key Points

- Courage is a strength rooted in trust and obedience to God's guidance.
- The angel armies of God fight for us in spiritual battles, providing unseen support.
- Biblical figures like Abraham and Esther exhibited courage through their obedience to God.
- Courage often means standing firm in our faith, even when the world around us is shaken.
- Jesus displayed ultimate courage by facing the cross, showing love and forgiveness.
- True courage is bolstered by God's promise to never leave us, ensuring that fear cannot overpower us.

Key Themes

- **Courage as a Divine Empowerment:** True courage is not simply human willpower but an empowerment from God, who strengthens us to face life's trials with boldness. Trusting in His promises enables us to stand firm, knowing that our battles are not fought alone.
- **Angelic Support in Spiritual Battles:** In the spiritual realm, God's angels are actively engaged on our behalf. This divine assistance reassures us of His unyielding commitment to our protection and victory, helping us overcome fear.
- **Examples of Courageous Faith:** The lives of Abraham and Esther show us courage through faithful obedience, even when the outcome was uncertain. Their bold actions inspire us to trust in God's plans, regardless of potential risks.
- **Jesus as the Ultimate Example of Courage:** Jesus modeled the highest form of courage by choosing the cross, embracing suffering out of love for humanity. His courage demonstrates a sacrificial love that compels us to face challenges with a forgiving and compassionate spirit.
- **Resilience in Trials and Endurance:** Scripture reminds us that trials develop perseverance, strengthening our courage and faith. We are called to respond with a sound mind and unwavering trust, knowing that God's spirit of power and love is within us.

Conclusion

Living courageously is about embracing God's strength and faithfulness, allowing His presence to dispel fear and uncertainty. We are emboldened by His promises and His constant companionship, knowing that His angels fight on our behalf. Let courage shape your life, driven by faith and trust in the God who goes before you. Step forward, knowing you are surrounded by His power and protected by His love.

CHAPTER 33

JOY

Bible Verse

Nehemiah 8:10 NIV - "Do not grieve, for the joy of
the Lord is your strength."

Introduction

True joy, deeper than fleeting happiness, is
rooted in our relationship with God and
sustained by the Holy Spirit's presence.
This chapter explores joy as a fruit of the Spirit
that fills and sustains us through life's challenges,
allowing us to experience His strength. Through a
shared journey in ministry, the author reflects on
moments of divine joy with mentor Tommy
Welchel, where joy transformed lives and left a
legacy of laughter, healing, and love.

Word of Wisdom

*"If you have no joy, there's a leak in
your Christianity somewhere." —Billy
Sunday*

Main Theme

Joy is a foundational attribute of faith, emanating from God's love and salvation. It is a spiritual strength that transcends circumstances, filling us with a sense of peace and enduring contentment.

Key Points

- Joy is rooted in a relationship with God and strengthened by His presence.
- It is an enduring heart posture, not dependent on our surroundings or situations.
- The joy of the Lord provides strength, offering resilience through challenges.
- Joy is deeply tied to the hope of salvation, inspiring an eternal perspective.
- Jesus' resurrection is the ultimate source of joy, conquering sin and death.
- Living joyfully attracts others to the beauty of God's love and peace.

Key Themes

- **Joy Beyond Circumstances:** Genuine joy is independent of life's ups and downs, anchored instead in the unwavering love and promises of God. This joy is a constant assurance that endures beyond temporary happiness.
- **The Strength Found in Joy:** Joy acts as a wellspring of strength, sustaining us through hardships and trials. The Bible

repeatedly affirms that joy strengthens us, fortifying us against weariness and despair.

- **The Divine Source of Joy:** Joy flows from God's presence and our communion with the Holy Spirit, filling our hearts as we draw closer to Him. The psalmist declares that the fullness of joy is found in God's presence, making intimacy with Him essential.
- **Joy as a Reflection of Faith:** Joy reflects our salvation and relationship with Jesus, bearing witness to His love. The resurrection of Christ underscores joy as a central reality of faith, bringing a lasting peace and hope that shines through us.
- **An Eternal Perspective on Joy:** Understanding our heavenly inheritance shifts our perspective from earthly troubles to eternal joy. Jesus encourages us to rejoice because our reward is in Heaven, transforming temporal struggles into reasons for gratitude.

Conclusion

Joy is not a fleeting sentiment but a gift that overflows from a heart anchored in God's promises. It sustains, empowers, and calls others to faith, marking the life of a believer with divine peace and strength. In every trial and triumph, joy points us back to the enduring reality of God's love and the assurance of eternity with Him. Embrace this joy, let it fill your life, and share its transformative light with others.

CHAPTER 34

INTERCESSION AND WARFARE

Bible Verse

Romans 8:27 ESV - "And he who searches hearts knows what is the mind of the Spirit, because the Spirit intercedes for the saints according to the will of God."

Introduction

Intercession and spiritual warfare are powerful expressions of prayer that engage believers in the defense and liberation of others, standing against the forces of darkness. This chapter highlights a powerful personal story of spiritual battle for a loved one, illustrating how God equips us with the strength and authority to fight for the spiritual well-being of others through prayer, faith, and discernment.

Word of Wisdom

"Satan trembles when he sees the

weakest saint upon their knees." —William Cowper

Main Theme

Intercession and warfare empower us to stand in the gap for others, enabling us to confront and overcome the forces of evil through the strength, authority, and guidance provided by God.

Key Points

• Intercession is an act of love, lifting others' needs to God with faith and expectancy.

• Spiritual warfare involves recognizing the battle between good and evil, often fought through prayer.

• Interceding requires spiritual discernment and an openness to God's guidance in prayer.

• Warfare is part of the Christian journey, equipping us to combat evil forces with God's armor.

• Prayer can break strongholds, heal, and restore, bringing freedom and peace to those in need.

• God calls us to be vigilant, using our authority to reclaim what the enemy seeks to take.

Key Themes

• **The Nature of Intercession:** Intercession is an act of selfless compassion, allowing us to connect with the struggles of others by bringing their needs before the Lord. This prayer cultivates a deeper connection to God's heart and allows us to participate in His work on earth.

- **Spiritual Warfare as a Form of Prayer:** Engaging in spiritual warfare means recognizing the reality of forces opposed to God's work and actively resisting them through prayer, Scripture, and the authority of Jesus. This battle is a critical part of faith, calling us to stand firm and rely on His strength.

- **Power in Corporate Intercession:** When believers join in prayer as a unified body, the spiritual impact is magnified. Jesus promises His presence when we gather, strengthening our prayers and establishing a sense of divine authority over evil.

- **Equipped with Divine Armor:** God provides spiritual armor for our protection, enabling us to stand against the enemy. Ephesians 6:12 emphasizes our battle is not against flesh but spiritual forces, reminding us that our faith and God's Word are our greatest defenses.

- **Victory Through Jesus' Authority:** Spiritual warfare isn't a solo effort; it relies on Christ's triumph over darkness. His authority assures us that our prayers are powerful, and as we engage in intercession and warfare, we do so from a place of promised victory.

Conclusion

Intercession and warfare are crucial tools for confronting the spiritual battles faced by those around us and within our communities. They reflect the heart of Christ, who intercedes for us, and empower us to stand with strength and conviction. Embrace the call to intercede with fervor and engage in spiritual warfare with confidence, knowing that God's promises assure our victory.

CHAPTER 35

PERSEVERANCE AND STEADFASTNESS

Bible Verse

Galatians 6:9 NIV - "Let us not become weary in doing good, for at the proper time we will reap a harvest if we do not give up."

Introduction

Perseverance and steadfastness are foundational virtues in the Christian walk, enabling believers to continue in faith, resist doubts, and trust in God's promises. This chapter recounts a journey marked by these virtues, illustrating how God's promises unfold when we remain unwavering in our faith and resolute in His calling.

Word of Wisdom

"Obstacles are those frightful things you see when you take your eyes off the goal." —Hannah More

Main Theme

Perseverance and steadfastness equip us to journey through trials with unwavering faith, helping us stay the course as we await God's promised blessings and divine timing.

Key Points

• Steadfastness is being deeply rooted in God's truth, holding firm against doubt.

• Perseverance is the enduring drive that propels us forward even when the outcome is unseen.

• Challenges test and build character, resulting in a hope that does not disappoint.

• The union of perseverance and steadfastness positions us to receive God's promises in His perfect time.

• Miracles are often birthed through the persistent and unwavering faith of believers.

• Trials can transform into testimonies of God's glory through steadfast commitment to Him.

Key Themes

• **Strength in Steadfastness:** A steadfast heart is deeply anchored in the promises and Word of God, allowing believers to withstand life's storms. This rootedness produces resilience, equipping us to remain unmoved by circumstances.

- **Perseverance as a Pathway to Victory:** Perseverance fuels the journey of faith, enabling us to push forward despite difficulties. This persistent spirit reflects a living hope in God's faithfulness and in His perfect timing for our breakthrough.
- **Miracles through Unyielding Faith:** Many miracles emerge as believers persistently trust in God's promises. This chapter illustrates how unwavering faith can attract the supernatural intervention of God in situations that seem impossible.
- **Endurance in the Early Church:** The apostles' unwavering perseverance and steadfastness amidst persecution serve as powerful examples. Their faith transformed trials into testimonies, fueling the growth and influence of the early church.
- **Perseverance and Character Development:** Romans 5:3-5 shows how suffering produces perseverance, which leads to character and hope. Through challenges, God strengthens our character, deepens our trust, and fills us with a hope that is both resilient and radiant.

Conclusion

Steadfastness and perseverance are vital to fulfilling our spiritual journey and receiving God's promises. As we hold fast to His Word, refusing to waver, we cultivate a resilient faith that ultimately invites God's presence and power into every part of our lives. With hearts rooted in these virtues, we can face trials with a victorious spirit, knowing our faith will be rewarded in God's perfect timing.

CHAPTER 36

FASTING

Bible Verse

Isaiah 58:6 NIV - "Is not this the kind of fasting I have chosen: to loose the chains of injustice and untie the cords of the yoke, to set the oppressed free and break every yoke?"

Introduction

This chapter explores the spiritual practice of fasting and its profound ability to draw us closer to God, break spiritual strongholds, and position us to receive divine revelations. Fasting is presented as more than just abstaining from food; it is a journey of spiritual enrichment that brings clarity, power, and a deeper connection to God's will.

Word of Wisdom

"Fasting reduces the power of self so that the Holy Spirit can do a more in-

tense work within us." —Bill Bright

Main Theme

Fasting is a powerful spiritual discipline that opens doors to deeper communion with God, amplifies the power of prayer, and aligns believers with His purposes.

Key Points

- Fasting is a deliberate sacrifice of physical needs to prioritize spiritual growth and communication with God.
- The practice intensifies prayer, increasing its impact and allowing for more profound answers.
- During fasting, our spiritual senses are heightened, making us more sensitive to the Holy Spirit's guidance.
- Both individual and corporate fasting have unique, impactful purposes in times of need or spiritual preparation.
- Jesus instructs us on the importance of fasting, indicating it as an essential part of a believer's life.
- Fasting with a sincere heart attracts God's presence, making room for miracles, revelations, and answered prayers.

Key Themes

- **The Purpose of Fasting:** Fasting is an act of devotion that demonstrates our dependence on God and a desire to hear

His voice more clearly. It involves setting aside physical comforts to grow spiritually and seek God's direction and intervention in our lives.

- **Fasting as Spiritual Fuel:** Fasting empowers and enhances our prayers, making them fervent and spiritually charged. By combining fasting with prayer, believers can break through barriers and create a powerful impact in the spiritual realm.

- **Personal and Corporate Fasting:** Both personal and corporate fasting are impactful; personal fasting draws us into a private, intimate connection with God, while corporate fasting, like Esther's fast, strengthens the faith and resolve of an entire community, amplifying collective prayers.

- **Joyful Fasting:** Jesus invites us to approach fasting with joy and expectancy, not sorrow. True fasting involves a celebratory aspect as we trust God's faithful response, making it a time of holy anticipation rather than mere self-denial.

- **Revelation and Spiritual Sensitivity:** Fasting sharpens our spiritual senses, thinning the veil between us and God's presence. During fasting, revelations and insights flow more readily as we position ourselves to receive from God, allowing Him to reveal His heart to us.

Conclusion

Fasting is a divine tool that strengthens our faith, intensifies our prayers, and draws us closer to God. Through this practice, believers experience an empowered, intimate walk with Christ, unlocking the miraculous and aligning with His divine will. Embrace fasting as an invitation to enter God's glory, deepen your spiritual roots, and witness the power of His presence in every area of your life.

CHAPTER 37

FAITH

Bible Verse

James 1:6 NIV - "But when you ask, you must believe and not doubt, because the one who doubts is like a wave of the sea, blown and tossed by the wind."

Introduction

This chapter discusses the essence of faith as a trust in God's promises, even when circumstances seem overwhelming. Through faith, believers can witness the miraculous in the midst of limitations and find the strength to face life's challenges with confidence and hope.

Word of Wisdom

"To trust God in the light is nothing. But trust Him in the dark—that is faith."
—C.H. Spurgeon

Main Theme

Faith is the confident trust in God's promises, enabling believers to move beyond natural limitations and experience His divine provision, peace, and strength.

Key Points

- Faith connects us to God's promises, turning impossibilities into testimonies of His provision.
- Real faith often requires courage to believe in God's solutions when circumstances seem impossible.
- Faith is foundational to salvation, as we are saved by grace through our belief in Jesus.
- True faith isn't just positive thinking; it's the assurance in God's unseen work and trust in His timing.
- When we align our expectations with faith, we invite God's miraculous intervention in every aspect of life.
- Faith in action fuels our spiritual journey and allows us to experience God's presence in transformative ways.

Key Themes

- **The Substance of Faith:** Faith is an active trust in God that enables us to step into the unseen and experience His reality. Hebrews 11:1 describes it as "confidence in what we hope for and assurance about what we do not see," highlighting its role as the foundation of our relationship with God.

- **Faith and Divine Provision:** Faith calls us to trust God even in practical needs, as demonstrated in miraculous events where God provides abundantly beyond what is possible in human terms. When we surrender our needs in faith, God shows His faithfulness.
- **Faith as Salvation's Pathway:** Faith is essential for salvation, bringing us into relationship with God and transforming our lives as we trust in Jesus' finished work. Through faith, we receive grace, healing, and eternal promises, anchoring us in hope.
- **Endurance through Faith:** Just as Peter's faith enabled him to walk on water, our faith strengthens us through life's storms, allowing us to stand firm when difficulties arise. Fixing our gaze on Jesus stabilizes us, even in adversity.
- **The Empowering Nature of Faith:** Faith enables us to experience God's power, wisdom, and presence. It moves us to act beyond human limitations, to pray with expectation, and to rely on the Holy Spirit's guidance in every step.

Conclusion

Faith is a profound spiritual gift that invites God's presence and power into every aspect of life. It is more than an inner belief; it is an active, unshakable trust in His promises that transforms our daily experiences. Let your faith be steadfast, allowing God to work in extraordinary ways in every moment.

CHAPTER 38

THANKFULNESS AND GRATEFULNESS

Bible Verse

2 Corinthians 2:14 NIV - "But thanks be to God, who always leads us as captives in Christ's triumphal procession and uses us to spread the aroma of the knowledge of him everywhere."

Introduction

This chapter delves into the transformative power of thankfulness and gratefulness, explaining how they are vital for a deep, fulfilling relationship with God. Through a personal journey of setting aside distractions to focus entirely on Jesus, the chapter illustrates how thankfulness elevates our spiritual lives and brings an enduring sense of peace, joy, and closeness to the Lord.

Word of Wisdom

"God intervenes in people's lives all the

time. But we seldom document the special, faith-building events." —Steve Saint

Main Theme

Thankfulness and gratefulness are essential attitudes that open our hearts to experience the fullness of God's blessings and presence, while transforming our outlook on life and drawing us closer to His love.

Key Points

- Thankfulness draws us into deeper communion with God, transforming everyday moments into encounters with His presence.
- Practicing gratitude helps us overcome negative emotions by cultivating love, joy, and compassion within our hearts.
- Thankfulness can act as a powerful form of worship, shifting our focus from what we lack to what we have in Him.
- Being grateful allows us to uplift others, becoming vessels of encouragement and hope in their lives.
- Gratitude in difficult times strengthens our faith, reminding us of God's faithfulness and unchanging love.
- Embracing gratitude as a lifestyle leads to a heart overflowing with joy, even amid challenges.

Key Themes

- **The Transformative Power of Gratitude:** Living with gratitude is a choice to focus on God's goodness, regardless of our circumstances. This attitude not only elevates our spirits but also attracts His blessings as we continually recognize His faithfulness in our lives.
- **Thankfulness as a Form of Worship:** Thankfulness is a spiritual practice that honors God by acknowledging His constant care and provision. As we give thanks, we align ourselves with His heart and reinforce our dependence on Him.
- **Gratitude in Difficult Times:** Gratitude strengthens our resilience, helping us find peace and purpose during trials. When we thank God even in hardship, we affirm our trust in His plan and experience His supernatural peace.
- **Expressing Gratitude to Others:** Gratitude extends beyond God to those around us, nurturing compassion and love. By expressing thankfulness to others, we become conduits of God's love, uplifting and strengthening those we encounter.
- **A Lifestyle of Gratefulness:** Making gratitude a daily practice shapes a positive outlook, allowing us to live in God's joy and peace. It becomes a testimony of His goodness, transforming how we see ourselves and others through His love.

Conclusion

Thankfulness and gratefulness are more than emotions; they are powerful spiritual disciplines that deepen our connection to God and bring His joy and peace into every corner of our lives. When we embrace gratitude fully, we step into a life radiating His glory, impacting both ourselves and those around us.

CHAPTER 39

PROPHECY

Bible Verse

2 Peter 1:21 NIV - "For prophecy never had its origin in the human will, but prophets, though human, spoke from God as they were carried along by the Holy Spirit."

Introduction

Prophecy, a gift imparted by the Holy Spirit, enables believers to speak words that inspire, guide, and reveal the heart of God. This chapter reflects on the power and purpose of prophecy, underscoring how it serves as a bridge to divine guidance and a reminder of God's promises. Through personal experience, prophecy was shown as a path to spiritual calling, encouraging believers to heed God's voice and use this gift for His glory.

Word of Wisdom

"Prophecy brings people into a revela-

tion of the glory that has been assigned to them." —Kris Vallotton

Main Theme

The gift of prophecy is a powerful expression of God's love and guidance, meant to encourage, comfort, and reveal His will for individuals and the Church, always aligning with the truth of Scripture.

Key Points

• Prophecy is a divine gift from the Holy Spirit, intended to strengthen, encourage, and comfort believers.

• True prophecy leads to spiritual growth, creating deeper connections with God and reinforcing faith.

• Prophecy is not only about foretelling future events but also includes offering words of encouragement and revelation.

• Jesus Christ is the ultimate fulfillment of prophecy, and all prophetic words should align with His nature and the Bible.

• The gift of prophecy must be used with humility and discernment, ensuring alignment with God's Word.

• Testing the spirits and seeking God's confirmation are essential when receiving and sharing prophetic words.

Key Themes

- **Prophecy as a Spiritual Gift for Encouragement and Growth:** Prophecy strengthens and builds up the Church, offering words that are deeply affirming and spiritually enriching. It draws us closer to God and cultivates greater faith as we receive His encouragement and guidance.
- **The Central Role of the Holy Spirit in Prophecy:** The Holy Spirit serves as the origin and guide for all true prophetic words, acting as a divine communicator. Believers who embrace this gift experience increased sensitivity to God's guidance and a closer relationship with Him.
- **Discernment in Receiving and Giving Prophecy:** Not every spiritual impression is a true prophecy from God. Believers are encouraged to test prophetic words, aligning them with Scripture, which is the ultimate standard of truth.
- **Jesus as the Fulfillment and Focus of Prophecy:** All prophecy ultimately points to Jesus, whose life, sacrifice, and teachings embody God's promises. Prophetic messages should draw believers closer to Him and reflect His character and will.
- **The Power of Prophecy to Transform and Empower:** Prophetic words have the potential to inspire, heal, and renew faith within believers. This transformative power is meant to glorify God and guide His people into greater spiritual maturity and purpose.

Conclusion

Prophecy is a divine gift that brings believers into a deeper revelation of God's love, His plans, and the call to walk in His ways. As we open our hearts to this gift, we must be mindful to use it with humility, discernment, and reverence for God's Word, allowing the Holy Spirit to guide us into truth. Through prophecy, we are reminded that we are each part of a larger plan, called to grow in intimacy with Jesus and to encourage one another in faith.

CHAPTER 40

SELF-CONTROL

Bible Verse

Proverbs 25:28 ESV - "A man without self-control is like a city broken into and left without walls."

Introduction

Self-control is the ability to exercise restraint over one's thoughts, words, and actions, especially when emotions run high. This chapter highlights a personal journey of practicing self-control in a challenging relational conflict and reveals the profound impact of obedience, humility, and restraint. Through this experience, the author learns that self-control not only guards against immediate reactions but also strengthens spiritual maturity and deepens one's relationship with God.

Word of Wisdom

"By constant self-discipline and self-control you can develop greatness of character." —Grenville Kleiser

Main Theme

Self-control is a fruit of the Spirit that allows believers to navigate challenging situations with wisdom and grace, relying on the Holy Spirit to overcome impulses and exercise humility.

Key Points

- Self-control involves intentionally restraining emotions and reactions to honor God.
- The practice of humility can be challenging but is essential for spiritual growth.
- The Holy Spirit prompts believers to reconcile and show kindness, even when it feels undeserved.
- Obedience to God's call may require actions that seem counterintuitive but ultimately lead to peace.
- Choosing self-control over impulsive reactions leads to spiritual maturity and personal freedom.
- God uses moments of self-control to reveal deeper aspects of His love and character to us.

Key Themes

- **The Essence of Self-Control as a Spiritual Discipline:** Self-control is a key part of Christian life, helping believers avoid the pitfalls of unchecked emotions. It encourages believers to make choices that are in line with God's will rather than immediate desires.

- **The Role of the Holy Spirit in Developing Self-Control:** This gift cannot be achieved solely by human willpower; it requires a continual reliance on the Holy Spirit. Through prayer and guidance, the Holy Spirit empowers believers to cultivate self-restraint.

- **Self-Control as a Pathway to Humility and Reconciliation:** True self-control often leads believers toward humility, where they are willing to forgive and seek peace. Taking the step to reconcile, even when it's difficult, can bring healing to both parties and reflects Jesus' heart for unity.

- **Internal and External Aspects of Self-Control:** Self-control encompasses more than just outward behavior; it also involves monitoring internal thoughts and desires. Practicing self-control in our minds ensures that our external actions align with God's will and character.

- **The Connection Between Self-Control and Spiritual Freedom:** While it may seem restrictive, self-control actually leads to greater freedom. By avoiding destructive impulses, believers can live in peace and strength, grounded in the assurance of God's guidance and wisdom.

Conclusion

Self-control is a vital element of spiritual maturity, empowering believers to act with wisdom, restraint, and grace. By allowing the Holy Spirit to guide our responses, we not only guard our hearts but also build a deeper, more peaceful connection with God. As we practice self-control, we reflect His love and discipline in our lives, finding freedom and strength in His presence.

CHAPTER 41

POWER

Bible Verse

Acts 1:8 NIV - "But you will receive power when the Holy Spirit comes on you; and you will be my witnesses in Jerusalem, and in all Judea and Samaria, and to the ends of the earth."

Introduction

This chapter explores the transformative power of the Holy Spirit bestowed upon believers, equipping them to act as vessels of God's miracles, strength, and authority. Through faith, prayer, and submission to the Spirit, believers can overcome challenges, experience healing, and share the gospel. The chapter illustrates that God's power is not only a gift but also a responsibility to be exercised in humility and with a desire to serve others.

Word of Wisdom

"With the power of God within us, we

*need never fear the powers around us." —
Woodrow Kroll*

Main Theme

The power of the Holy Spirit is a dynamic force within every believer, enabling them to live with authority, overcome challenges, perform miracles, and bring God's Kingdom to those in need.

Key Points

- Power is a divine gift from God, designed for use in advancing His Kingdom and glorifying Him.
- The Holy Spirit's power enables believers to experience and impart miraculous healings and spiritual breakthroughs.
- Baptism in the Holy Spirit equips believers with spiritual gifts, strengthening their faith and boldness.
- True power requires humility and should be used for the benefit of others rather than self-gain.
- Through Christ, believers hold authority over the enemy, empowered to confront spiritual strongholds and bring freedom.
- This power is the same force that raised Jesus from the dead and dwells in every follower of Christ.

Key Themes

- **Source of All Power:** God the Father is the source of all power and authority, and His strength flows through us when we submit to Him. This divine empowerment enables us to act in ways that reflect His love, authority, and grace.
- **Empowerment Through the Holy Spirit:** Baptism in the Holy Spirit is an encounter that deepens believers' spiritual gifts and strengthens their faith. Walking in His might is about yielding to and partnering with the Holy Spirit, who equips us with courage and resilience.
- **Responsibility in Power:** Power is both a gift and a test of character, requiring believers to use it for uplifting others. Genuine authority, rooted in God, is not for personal gain but for serving others with compassion, humility, and integrity.
- **Spiritual Warfare and Victory:** Believers are engaged in spiritual warfare, armed with the power of prayer and God's Word. The Holy Spirit's presence within us gives us boldness and victory over darkness, enabling us to break chains of oppression and bring freedom through Christ.
- **Power That Transforms Lives:** The Holy Spirit empowers us to become witnesses of God's glory, acting as vessels of healing and deliverance. The power within us transforms our own lives and allows us to bring hope, healing, and the gospel to others.

Conclusion

The power of the Holy Spirit is a profound gift that transforms believers into conduits of God's grace, strength, and miracles. By understanding and embracing this power, we are called to live boldly, confront spiritual challenges, and bring God's Kingdom to those in need. The same power that raised Jesus from the dead resides in us, empowering us to live victorious lives that glorify God and bring hope to the world.

CHAPTER 42

COMMUNION

Bible Verse

Matthew 26:26-28 NIV - "While they were eating, Jesus took bread, and when he had given thanks, he broke it and gave it to his disciples, saying, 'Take and eat; this is my body.' Then he took a cup, and when he had given thanks, he gave it to them, saying, 'Drink from it, all of you. This is my blood of the covenant, which is poured out for many for the forgiveness of sins.'"

Introduction

Communion, a profound practice instituted by Jesus, allows believers to reflect on His sacrifice and connect deeply with His presence. This chapter illustrates how taking Communion opens the door to divine encounters and heavenly protection, as seen in moments of miraculous revelation and angelic visitation. Embracing Communion with a heart of gratitude brings believers into a closer relationship with God, renewing faith and intimacy with Him.

Word of Wisdom

"Jesus, I remember." Jody Keck

Main Theme

Communion is an act of remembrance and reverence for Jesus' ultimate sacrifice, creating a sacred connection between believers and God, deepening faith, and inviting His divine presence into our lives.

Key Points

- Communion connects us to Jesus' sacrifice, enabling us to remember His love and devotion.
- The practice began at the Last Supper and is now a shared symbol of unity within the body of Christ.
- Each time we take Communion, we invite God's presence and open ourselves to heavenly encounters.
- Communion is a time of self-reflection, calling us to examine our hearts and intentions.
- This sacrament provides an opportunity for personal renewal, acknowledging our dependence on Him.
- Communion can be taken individually or corporately, each time as an act of worship and remembrance.

Key Themes

- **Historical and Spiritual Foundation of Communion:** Communion was established at the Last Supper, representing Jesus' body and blood as a covenant with humanity. This sacrament, based on His teachings, invites believers to remember His sacrifice and promises until His return.
- **Personal and Collective Reflection:** Taking Communion offers a moment for deep introspection, allowing believers to come humbly before God. It encourages reconciliation with others and a personal commitment to grow in our walk with Christ.
- **Invitation to Intimacy with God:** Communion is an expression of our dedication to Jesus and invites His tangible presence into our lives. Through this practice, believers often experience a profound awareness of God's love and grace, deepening their relationship with Him.
- **Unity Within the Body of Christ:** When we partake in Communion, we join together with other believers, acknowledging that we are one in faith and purpose. It's a reminder of our shared identity in Christ and a call to walk in harmony with each other.
- **Healing, Renewal, and Divine Encounters:** Through Communion, believers may experience physical and spiritual healing, as well as moments of

divine revelation. This act of remembrance is a powerful way to renew faith, drawing upon the Holy Spirit's power for restoration and insight.

Conclusion

Communion is a sacred act that unites believers in the remembrance of Jesus' sacrifice, fostering intimacy with God and promoting unity within the church. Each time we take Communion, whether alone or with others, we honor Jesus' sacrifice and renew our commitment to Him. This holy practice opens the door to God's presence, bringing healing, spiritual renewal, and a deeper connection to His divine love.

CHAPTER 43

BOLDNESS

Bible Verse

Proverbs 28:1 ESV - "The wicked flee when no one pursues, but the righteous are bold as a lion."

Introduction

Boldness in faith is a steadfast courage that is born from an intimate trust in God's promises. This chapter illustrates how a quiet whisper from God led to an international calling, revealing that boldness emerges not from our own abilities, but from our willingness to trust in the vastness of His plans. Through acts of obedience and openness to His direction, believers can step into bold assignments with the confidence that God's power is behind them.

Word of Wisdom

"You don't have to beg God; you just

have to act upon His word." —F.F. Bosworth

Main Theme

Boldness is rooted in unwavering faith and reliance on God's guidance, enabling us to accomplish great things for His glory by taking courageous steps in obedience to His voice.

Key Points

• Boldness in faith is not recklessness but arises from a confident trust in God.

• Being bold allows us to act on divine assignments even when they seem beyond our natural capacity.

• Biblical figures like David and Paul exemplify boldness that is rooted in God's power rather than personal strength.

• Boldness enables us to be fearless witnesses of God's love and truth in a world often dominated by fear.

• To be bold is to be a vessel of God's power, ready to act in faith for His purposes.

• Boldness calls us to action, encouraging us to step out in faith and make an impact for the Kingdom.

Key Themes

• **Confidence in God's Power:** Boldness stems from a trust that God's power will accomplish what He has spoken, as seen in the life of David facing Goliath. True boldness is built on the assurance that God is faithful to His promises and equips us to face even the greatest challenges.

- **Approaching God with Assurance:** Boldness includes approaching God's throne with confidence, as stated in Hebrews 4:16, allowing us to find mercy and grace. This assurance builds our relationship with Him, fostering a courage that encourages us to seek and receive from Him fearlessly.

- **Testimonies of Bold Faith:** Christian martyrs and apostles like Paul serve as testimonies of bold faith, showing that standing firm in God's truth often requires bold actions. Their lives remind us that boldness can mean sacrificing comfort for the sake of spreading the Gospel and living out faith unashamedly.

- **Boldness as Action and Witness:** Boldness is both speaking and acting in faith, stepping out of comfort zones, and sharing the Gospel with confidence. In times of fear and uncertainty, boldness in Christ sets believers apart, allowing them to serve as beacons of hope and truth.

- **Holy Spirit Empowerment:** Paul's boldness on his missionary journeys highlights the essential role of the Holy Spirit's power in courageously facing opposition. Boldness is not self-generated; it's a divine gift, grounded in God's Spirit and aimed at furthering His Kingdom.

Conclusion

Boldness is a spiritual gift, rooted in faith and empowered by the Holy Spirit, allowing believers to live out their calling with courage and strength. By embracing boldness, we honor God's power and declare our trust in His promises. Living boldly for Him is a declaration that we are His vessels, ready to make an impact for the Kingdom. Let your boldness in Him be the key that opens doors to His presence, power, and purpose in your life.

CHAPTER 44

SACRIFICE AND DISCIPLINE

Bible Verse

Hebrews 13:16 NIV - "And do not forget to do good and to share with others, for with such sacrifices God is pleased."

Introduction

Sacrifice and discipline are twin expressions of a heart fully surrendered to God, intertwined as a response to His boundless love. In times of exhaustion or challenge, these virtues become avenues through which we honor God and serve others, fueled by His strength rather than our own. Through personal testimonies of sacrifice and the rewards of obedience, we see how God's power flows most profoundly when we yield ourselves entirely to His purposes.

Word of Wisdom

"If Jesus Christ be God and died for me, then no sacrifice can be too great for me to make for Him." —Charles Studd

Main Theme

Sacrifice and discipline go hand-in-hand as acts of devotion to God, reflecting both our love for Him and our commitment to living out His calling with integrity and perseverance.

Key Points

• Sacrifice is an expression of love and gratitude to God, drawing us closer to Him.

• Discipline is a purposeful, joyful pursuit of God's presence and a means to strengthen faith.

• Sacrifice sometimes means surrendering personal comforts for the sake of others' well-being and the Kingdom.

• Discipline is not only about routines but about cultivating a heart eager to connect with God.

• Both sacrifice and discipline are empowered by the Holy Spirit, who strengthens us beyond our limitations.

• Through sacrifice and discipline, we reflect Christ's example of selflessness and commitment to God's will.

Key Themes

- **Sacrifice as a Response to God's Love:** Sacrifice flows from an appreciation of God's love, as seen in Jesus' ultimate sacrifice on the cross. This selflessness mirrors the compassion of Christ, enabling us to reflect His love in our daily actions toward others.

- **Discipline as Joyful Devotion:** True discipline is a reflection of our deep devotion to God and is more than a rigid routine; it's a joyful and consistent pursuit of Him. Through daily prayer, worship, and reading the Word, we deepen our relationship and strengthen our spiritual lives.

- **Surrendering Control to God's Will:** Sacrifice involves releasing our own desires to fulfill God's higher purposes. Surrender is an act of trust that allows the Holy Spirit to guide our lives, making space for Him to work through us in ways we cannot foresee.

- **The Power of Spirit-Filled Discipline:** Discipline, under the Holy Spirit's guidance, becomes a force that draws us to a greater knowledge of God and a clearer understanding of His will. It sharpens our focus on His voice, aligning our hearts with His purpose and granting us resilience.

- **Emulating Christ's Selflessness:** As followers of Christ, both sacrifice and discipline allow us to emulate His humility and selflessness. These virtues are vital for growth, shaping us to become more like Him and empowering us to serve as His hands and feet.

Conclusion

Sacrifice and discipline are powerful tools that reflect our commitment to God's call and enable us to live in deeper communion with Him. By laying aside our desires and embracing a life of devotion, we position ourselves as vessels for God's power and love. In moments of weariness, these virtues remind us that God's strength is perfected in our weakness, allowing us to fulfill His purposes with joy and gratitude. Embrace sacrifice and discipline as paths to spiritual growth, knowing they are keys to a life that glorifies God.

CHAPTER 45

MERCY

Bible Verse

Micah 6:8 NIV - "He has shown you, O mortal, what is good. And what does the Lord require of you? To act justly and to love mercy and to walk humbly with your God."

Introduction

Mercy is the expression of God's deep compassion and loving forgiveness, a gift we're called to extend to others as we grow in faith. Through a personal story, this chapter highlights the powerful impact of showing mercy, even in small, seemingly insignificant moments, and how choosing mercy can deepen our relationship with God and transform how we see others.

Word of Wisdom

"The deepest passion of the heart of Jesus was not the saving of men, but the glory of God; and then the saving of men, because that is for the glory of God." —G. Campbell Morgan

Main Theme

Mercy is not only an act of forgiveness but a testament to God's unconditional love and grace, encouraging us to reflect His heart and see the beauty in all of His creation.

Key Points

• Mercy is central to the Father's love for us and a powerful invitation to reflect that love toward others.

• Acts of mercy strengthen our relationship with God and build a bridge of understanding and compassion.

• Jesus' life exemplifies mercy, extending grace to those considered unworthy and demonstrating that mercy is a blessing to both giver and receiver.

• Mercy requires seeing beyond a person's actions to the heart beneath, allowing us to offer true compassion.

• Practicing mercy fosters humility and allows us to walk in alignment with God's will.

• Mercy is an active choice that blesses and uplifts others, even those who may not seem deserving.

Key Themes

- **God's Mercy as a Model for Us:** God's unmerited mercy toward us sets a standard for how we are to treat others. His forgiveness and love call us to view each person as His creation, deserving of dignity and compassion.
- **Jesus' Example of Mercy in Action:** Jesus spent time with those on the margins, extending mercy beyond societal expectations. His actions remind us that mercy should extend beyond mere forgiveness to active kindness and empathy.
- **Mercy as Strength in Humility:** Extending mercy demonstrates a deep inner strength and humility. True mercy goes against the grain of judgment and anger, creating a space for healing and understanding.
- **Mercy's Power to Transform Relationships:** Choosing mercy over judgment has the power to heal and restore relationships. By following Christ's example, we become vessels for reconciliation and redemption.
- **Mercy as a Conduit for Spiritual Growth:** Embracing mercy opens us to a closer walk with God, cultivating a heart that reflects His love. As we practice mercy, we grow in our capacity for

empathy and deepen our understanding of God's grace.

Conclusion

Mercy, in all its forms, is a gift that allows us to reflect God's boundless compassion. As we embrace mercy, we align our hearts with His and become vessels of His love, grace, and forgiveness. Every act of mercy is an invitation to connect more deeply with the Father and to embody the transformative power of His love. Walk in mercy, allowing it to shape your character and inspire those around you.

CHAPTER 46

HOPE

Bible Verse

Romans 15:13 NIV - "May the God of hope fill you with all joy and peace as you trust in him, so that you may overflow with hope by the power of the Holy Spirit."

Introduction

Hope is a powerful assurance anchored in God's faithfulness, guiding us through life's uncertainties with a confidence rooted in His promises. This chapter shares a personal journey of overcoming fear through hope, demonstrating how steadfast trust in God can transform challenges into testimonies of His love and presence.

Word of Wisdom

"The hope that God has provided for you is not merely a wish. Neither is it

dependent on other people, possessions, or circumstances for its validity. Instead, biblical hope is an application of your faith that supplies a confident expectation in God's fulfillment of His promises."
—John Broger

Main Theme

Hope, grounded in faith and rooted in God's promises, gives us a steadfast assurance that strengthens us to face life's trials with peace and confidence in His timing and purposes.

Key Points

• True hope in God gives us a steady anchor amidst life's storms, rooted in His unchanging character.

• Hope connects us to eternal life through Jesus, bringing peace in our current journey and confidence for the future.

• Biblical hope is not wishful thinking; it's a confident expectation of God's promises fulfilled.

• This assurance sustains us, allowing us to remain joyful even when circumstances appear uncertain.

• The Scriptures consistently highlight hope as a source of strength and comfort, encouraging us to lean on God in all things.

• Hope shapes our identity, infusing us with a spirit of endurance, perseverance, and trust.

Key Themes

- **Hope as an Anchor in Life:** Hope steadies our souls, giving us an unwavering trust in God's character. It reassures us that He will fulfill His promises, even when challenges arise.
- **The Power of Persistent Prayer in Hope:** When we pray, our hope is strengthened, connecting us with God's heart and aligning us with His will. The act of prayer not only seeks answers but reinforces our trust in His divine timing.
- **Hope Rooted in God's Promises:** Hope is not based on fleeting circumstances but on the enduring truth of God's promises. Verses like Jeremiah 29:11 remind us that God has plans to prosper us, offering a future filled with hope.
- **Hope in Waiting:** Hope teaches us patience, inviting us to trust in God's perfect timing. As we wait with expectation, we build spiritual resilience, learning that God's answers are always timely and purposeful.
- **Hope in the Eternal Perspective:** Hope draws our eyes to the future glory that awaits, far surpassing present difficulties. This eternal perspective helps us face challenges with courage and a forward-looking vision grounded in Jesus.

Conclusion

Hope is an essential part of our spiritual lives, a divine gift that fuels us with joy and peace as we trust in God. It is a confident assurance that He is with us, leading us with purpose and grace. Let hope become your guiding light, knowing that it is a key to understanding God's promises and embracing the future He has prepared for you. Never lose hope; it is the foundation of His presence and a vital connection to His power in your life.

CHAPTER 47

RECONCILIATION

Bible Verse

Matthew 5:23-24 NIV - "Therefore, if you are offering your gift at the altar and there remember that your brother or sister has something against you, leave your gift there in front of the altar. First go and be reconciled to them; then come and offer your gift."

Introduction

Reconciliation is a profound act of restoring relationships, rooted in God's desire for unity and peace. This chapter reflects on a personal experience where God prompted an act of reconciliation, reminding us that initiating healing is a mark of genuine love for Him. In choosing to make things right, even when not at fault, we reflect the humility and compassion of Christ.

Word of Wisdom

"The one who loves Me the most will be the first one to make it right."

Main Theme

Reconciliation calls us to follow God's example of grace, initiating peace, and healing in our relationships, regardless of blame, to reflect the depth of our love for Him and commitment to unity.

Key Points

• Reconciliation is an invitation to love like Christ, putting aside pride to restore broken relationships.

• Loving God wholeheartedly means prioritizing peace and taking the first step to mend conflicts.

• Forgiveness is an essential component of reconciliation, allowing us to release burdens and find healing.

• The Holy Spirit guides us toward reconciliation, revealing areas where we need to restore harmony.

• Reconciliation requires humility and surrender, reflecting our willingness to prioritize others' well-being.

• This process ultimately leads to inner peace and aligns our hearts with God's will for unity.

Key Themes

- **Reflecting God's Grace Through Reconciliation:** In forgiving others, we mirror God's own forgiveness, acknowledging our shared human imperfections. The act of reconciliation is a visible expression of His mercy and unconditional love.
- **Humility in Restoration:** True reconciliation requires humility, acknowledging that our love for God should motivate us to mend relationships, even when it's difficult. This humility empowers us to extend peace, regardless of fault.
- **Empowered by the Holy Spirit:** Reconciliation is a divine process, guided by the Holy Spirit. His gentle leading enables us to approach strained relationships with compassion and an open heart, seeking God's will for peace.
- **Faith and Open Communication:** Reconciliation involves honest, respectful conversations that seek understanding over argument. By listening carefully and responding thoughtfully, we embody Christ's approach to healing conflicts.
- **The Continuous Journey of Forgiveness and Restoration:** Reconciliation is not always a return to previous relationship dynamics; sometimes, it's about moving forward with renewed boundaries and grace. Through prayer and courage, God's peace guides the way.

Conclusion

Reconciliation is a transformative practice that embodies God's love and seeks to restore what's been broken. By choosing to reconcile, we reflect Jesus' heart for unity and peace, setting aside personal grievances to honor Him. With the Holy Spirit's guidance, let reconciliation become a key in your walk with Christ, anchoring you in His peace and love as you extend grace to others.

CHAPTER 48

CHARACTER

Bible Verse

1 Corinthians 15:33 NIV - "Do not be misled: 'Bad company corrupts good character.'"

Introduction

Character is foundational to spiritual growth and effective leadership, aligning us with God's standards, regardless of the cost. In this chapter, the author recounts an experience counseling church leaders on the importance of integrity and spiritual maturity, illustrating how compromises in character can lead to spiritual turmoil. The guidance provided highlights that a life of holy character serves as our greatest defense against spiritual challenges and a testimony of God's transforming work in us.

Word of Wisdom

"The one who loves Me the most will be the first one to make it right."

Main Theme

True character, anchored in God's principles, protects against spiritual pitfalls and empowers us to serve faithfully, influencing others through the integrity and strength of our actions.

Key Points

• Character reflects our relationship with God and is an outward testimony of His work in us.

• Integrity in leadership is essential for spiritual maturity and guidance within the church.

• Compromising character leaves "chinks in the armor," which weaken our spiritual defenses.

• True character is rooted in humility and a commitment to holiness, guided by the Holy Spirit.

• God's armor, paired with solid character, helps us withstand the enemy's subtle schemes.

• Cultivating Christlike character requires ongoing surrender and obedience to His will.

Key Themes

- **Integrity in Leadership:** Leaders with strong character influence others positively, upholding standards that bring glory to God and prevent division within the church. When leadership lacks maturity, spiritual weakness seeps into the congregation.

- **The Heart as the Foundation of Character:** Our character originates from our hearts, influencing our words, actions, and treatment of others. A pure heart reflects God's love through kindness, honesty, and compassion.
- **The Armor of God and Spiritual Warfare:** Character plays a crucial role in spiritual resilience, enabling us to "put on the armor of God" to resist the devil's schemes. A strong character guards against subtle influences that lead to moral decay and compromised faith.
- **Testing and Refinement:** Life's trials test and shape our character, teaching reliance on God's strength and wisdom. Facing challenges with integrity strengthens us spiritually and builds our capacity to overcome.
- **The Power of Character in Witness:** A character rooted in Christ serves as a powerful witness to God's goodness, attracting others to faith. When we live out integrity and compassion, we reflect God's nature, drawing people closer to Him.

Conclusion

Character, deeply rooted in God's principles, equips us to live a life that honors Him, strengthens our spiritual defenses, and enables us to lead with integrity and humility. Through intentional surrender and reliance on the Holy Spirit, character becomes the key to a life that testifies of God's love, drawing others to experience His transformative power. Let your character shine brightly, glorifying Jesus and impacting the world for His Kingdom.

CHAPTER 49

ALERTNESS AND READINESS

Bible Verse

1 Peter 5:8 NIV - "Be alert and of sober mind. Your enemy the devil prowls around like a roaring lion looking for someone to devour."

Introduction

This chapter highlights the importance of being spiritually alert and ready to act when called upon. The author recounts a dramatic experience in which a young life was saved through prayer, emphasizing the necessity of vigilance in our relationship with God. The Holy Spirit calls us to a state of constant readiness, prepared to respond with faith and authority in any situation.

Word of Wisdom

"Be ready! What I'm calling you to do,

you won't have time to get ready, you have to be ready."

Main Theme

Alertness and readiness empower believers to respond promptly to God's call, staying spiritually prepared to act with wisdom and authority against the enemy's schemes.

Key Points

• God calls us to be spiritually vigilant, prepared to respond at any moment.

• Readiness comes through consistent practices like prayer, Bible study, and fasting.

• Jesus emphasized watchfulness and preparedness in His teachings.

• The parable of the talents teaches us to wisely invest our God-given abilities.

• Spiritual preparation is essential for keeping God's light burning brightly in us.

• Discernment and vigilance help us guard against deception and complacency.

Key Themes

• **Spiritual Vigilance:** Alertness in faith keeps us ready to act swiftly when God calls. This vigilance is rooted in close fellowship with the Holy Spirit, attuning us to His guidance.

- **Preparedness in Action:** Being prepared spiritually allows us to confront crises with faith and authority. Through readiness, we can stand firm and respond confidently to challenges, fully equipped in His strength.
- **Using Our Gifts Wisely:** Jesus' parable of the talents reminds us to actively use and invest the gifts we're given. Readiness involves a commitment to serve and share what God has entrusted to us.
- **The Importance of Oil in Our Lamps:** The parable of the ten virgins underscores the need for spiritual preparation and anointing. Our readiness is symbolized by keeping our spiritual "lamps" filled with the Holy Spirit's presence.
- **Guarding Against Complacency and Temptation:** Discernment helps us stay vigilant, recognizing and resisting the enemy's schemes. Spiritual readiness includes protecting our hearts from distractions and falsehoods.

Conclusion

Alertness and readiness are vital attributes that empower us to walk closely with the Holy Spirit, ever prepared for His calling. Just as the author experienced a moment of divine intervention, we too are called to live with our hearts open and spirits stirred, expectant and ready for God's direction. Remain vigilant, attuned to His voice, and willing to act when He calls—transforming the ordinary into the extraordinary through His power and presence.

CHAPTER 50

IDENTITY

Bible Verse

Genesis 1:27 NIV - "So God created mankind in his own image, in the image of God he created them; male and female he created them."

Introduction

This chapter explores the essence of our identity as rooted in God's love, portraying the divine worth and purpose He has placed in each of us. The author recounts a moment when she felt God's personal affirmation of her value, illustrating how deeply and individually He knows and loves us. Embracing our identity in Him changes how we see ourselves and how we relate to others.

Word of Wisdom

"He wants us to know our identity is

in Him! We are fearfully and wonderfully made, created in His image." Jody Keck

Main Theme

Our identity is founded in the image of God and His love for us, offering a profound sense of purpose, dignity, and belonging that transcends external standards.

Key Points

• God created us in His image, imparting inherent worth and beauty.

• Our identity is confirmed through Jesus' sacrifice, aligning us with God's purpose.

• As heirs with Christ, our relationship with Him shapes our identity and worth.

• True identity in Christ brings freedom from guilt, shame, and worldly comparisons.

• Our identity isn't defined by our efforts but by God's love and grace.

• We are designed to reflect God's love, living as His masterpieces with purpose.

Key Themes

• **Image of God as Our Foundation:**
Recognizing ourselves as created in His

image affirms our inherent worth and dignity. This divine imprint shapes our identity, purpose, and relationships with others, reflecting God's love and grace.

- **New Creation in Christ:** Through faith in Jesus, we become new creations, leaving behind the burdens of guilt and shame. Our rebirth into this identity frees us to live joyfully and confidently in the grace He offers.
- **Grace-Based Identity:** Our identity in Christ doesn't rely on our own actions or achievements but rests on His love and mercy. This truth fosters humility, anchoring us in God's grace rather than self-sufficiency.
- **Unique and Purposeful Design:** Ephesians 2:10 declares us God's handiwork, created with purpose and value. This purpose aligns us with His Kingdom work, encouraging us to use our gifts in service to others and glorify Him.
- **Belonging Without Comparison:** In a world of comparisons, our identity in Christ stands as a secure foundation, grounded in being His beloved. This perspective frees us from external pressures, allowing us to embrace who we are in Him.

Conclusion

Embracing our identity in Christ fills our lives with purpose, belonging, and joy. As His masterpieces, we are called to walk in the assurance of His love, living in alignment with His plans and reflecting His glory. When we know who we are in Him, we experience the fullness of life as God intended, living confidently as His children, deeply loved and cherished.

CHAPTER 51

HOSPITALITY

Bible Verse

1 Peter 4:9-10 NIV - "Offer hospitality to one another without grumbling. Each of you should use whatever gift you have received to serve others, as faithful stewards of God's grace in its various forms."

Introduction

This chapter unfolds the profound significance of hospitality, showing how opening our hearts and homes to others can become a gateway for divine encounters and blessings. The author shares a transformative experience of hosting Tommy Welchel, whose stories of the Azusa Street Revival ignited a deeper sense of purpose. Through this encounter, hospitality became a channel for spiritual inheritance and a powerful demonstration of God's grace.

Word of Wisdom

"Hospitality had become a gateway for a divine encounter." Jody Keck

Main Theme

Hospitality is more than an act of hosting; it's an extension of God's love that creates space for spiritual connection, healing, and growth.

Key Points

• Hospitality is an invitation to bring God's love and grace to others.

• Jesus exemplified ultimate hospitality by sharing meals and time with people from all walks of life.

• Welcoming others fosters belonging and encourages genuine connection.

• Biblical hospitality often leads to divine encounters and unforeseen blessings.

• Practicing hospitality is a continuous act of service to others, as emphasized in Romans 12:13.

• Hospitality, when offered sincerely, reflects the heart of Jesus and the essence of Christian love.

Key Themes

• **Divine Encounters Through Hospitality:** Opening our homes can lead to meaningful spiritual moments, as exemplified by the author's encounter with

Tommy Welchel, which unveiled a deeper calling. This experience shows that by welcoming others, we might also be welcoming divine assignments.

- **Jesus as the Model of Hospitality:** Jesus' openness to dining with people of all backgrounds exemplifies true hospitality. His parable of the great banquet encourages us to invite those who may not be able to reciprocate, showing kindness without expectation.
- **Creating Spaces of Belonging and Connection:** Hospitality fosters a sense of belonging by offering a safe and welcoming space where people can be themselves. This approach creates opportunities for connection, empathy, and understanding of diverse perspectives.
- **Biblical Examples of Unexpected Blessings:** Abraham and Sarah's welcoming of three strangers, who turned out to be angels, demonstrates the divine potential in every act of hospitality. This story highlights the blessings that often follow when we welcome others wholeheartedly.
- **Continuous Practice of Hospitality:** Romans 12:13 calls us to practice hospitality as a consistent and genuine act of faith, not as a one-time gesture. This practice cultivates a servant heart, emphasizing the importance of opening our hearts and homes regularly as an expression of God's grace.

Conclusion

Hospitality, rooted in love and service, opens the door to divine encounters and makes God's love tangible. When we welcome others, we reflect Jesus' own example, creating spaces of acceptance, kindness, and spiritual depth. Embrace hospitality as a continuous expression of faith, knowing that each act has the potential to make God's love real to others and bring unexpected blessings.

CHAPTER 52

PATIENCE

Bible Verse

Proverbs 15:18 NIV - "A hot-tempered person stirs up conflict, but the one who is patient calms a quarrel."

Introduction

Patience, a vital fruit of the Spirit, is more than just waiting—it's an active demonstration of faith and trust in God's timing. The author shares an experience of trusting God's timing and moving from a season of waiting to active participation in His work. This chapter highlights the strength that patience gives, enabling believers to endure, trust, and experience God's promises.

Word of Wisdom

"Don't settle for being an observer— become a partaker." Jody Keck

Main Theme

Patience is the enduring faith that sustains us through seasons of waiting, enabling us to persevere and grow spiritually as we trust in God's timing.

Key Points

• Patience requires a calm trust in God's timing, which often differs from our own.

• Through patience, we build reliance on God's guidance, allowing His promises to come to pass.

• Waiting is an opportunity for spiritual growth, refining our character and fortifying our faith.

• Patience shifts us from passive observation to active participation in God's work.

• The Bible encourages patience as a means of cultivating unity, forgiveness, and resilience in relationships.

• God's patience with us is a model for the patience we should extend to ourselves and others.

Key Themes

• **Patience as Active Trust:** Patience is not passive; it is an active reliance on God's wisdom and timing. This trust acknowledges that His plans, though sometimes delayed by our understanding, are always purposeful and perfect.

- **Growth Through Waiting:** God uses periods of waiting to develop and refine our character. Like the author's experience, the waiting process can transition us from observers to active participants in His promises, deepening our faith and understanding.
- **Patience in Relationships:** Practicing patience with others fosters unity, understanding, and love. Ephesians 4:2 calls us to bear with each other in love, a reminder that patience enhances our connections and strengthens forgiveness.
- **The Example of Jesus' Patience:** Jesus' life exemplifies patience through sacrificial love and obedience to God's will. His steadfast endurance serves as our ultimate model, encouraging us to navigate life's challenges with a similar strength grounded in divine trust.
- **Patience as a Reflection of Maturity:** Romans emphasizes that patient hope is a mark of spiritual maturity. As we wait for unseen promises, patience develops our resilience and faith, preparing us to embrace His will

Conclusion

Patience is a profound expression of trust in God, shaping us to endure challenges with grace and purpose. This gift equips us to navigate life's uncertainties with calm assurance and to engage fully in God's work when His timing aligns. Embrace patience as both a strength and a discipline, and trust that in waiting, we are refined, prepared, and ultimately blessed by His perfect plan.

CHAPTER 53

SERVICE AND FRUITFULNESS

Bible Verse

Matthew 5:16 NIV - "In the same way, let your light shine before others, that they may see your good deeds and glorify your Father in heaven."

Introduction

Service and fruitfulness are intertwined expressions of a life devoted to God. In this chapter, the author recounts a dream in which butterflies symbolize transformation, purpose, and hope, representing a future marked by a divine calling to service. This chapter emphasizes that, as we serve God and others, our lives will bear fruit that glorifies Him and impacts others profoundly.

Word of Wisdom

"Serve Him for all your days, and you

growth. As we embrace God's call to serve, our actions become a testimony of His love and compassion. Rooted in the Holy Spirit, our lives will bear fruit that endures, spreading the message of His Kingdom and transforming lives. Embrace this call, letting God's presence guide you in love and abundance.

CHAPTER 54

ENDING

Bible Verse

Revelation 22:17 NIV - "The Spirit and the bride say, 'Come!' And let the one who hears say, 'Come!' Let the one who is thirsty come; and let the one who wishes take the free gift of the water of life."

Introduction

This chapter provides a glimpse of God's eternal Kingdom, portrayed through John's vision of the river of life flowing from God's throne. This river represents God's eternal promise, an invitation to all believers to drink from the waters of life and find healing, redemption, and peace in His presence. As the book concludes, readers are urged to make a choice: to live fully in God's presence and pursue holiness, or remain adrift without direction.

Word of Wisdom

"You are not a visitation, but a habitation of God. Seek Him and be a vessel of His glory in this final hour." Jody Keck

Main Theme

The final chapter is a call to fully embrace God's presence, walking in holiness and living a life dedicated to His glory. It reminds us that we are created for His eternal kingdom, and invites us to live in the fullness of His promises and power.

Key Points

• John's vision of the river of life reveals God's eternal covenant of grace and redemption.

• We are given the choice to embrace God's presence or remain adrift in life's uncertainties.

• Living in God's presence means being a habitation, not merely a visitor, of His Spirit.

• Holiness and readiness are essential for ushering in revival and experiencing God's glory.

• Reflecting on these keys encourages a deeper commitment to spiritual growth and God's call.

• The journey does not end here; believers are urged to continue walking in God's power and love.

Key Themes

- **The River of Life as God's Eternal Promise:** John's vision of the river flowing from God's throne symbolizes His grace and redemption for all who come to drink. This river is filled with life, healing, and the brilliance of His glory, representing the promise of eternal fellowship with the Creator.
- **Our Role as Habitations of God's Presence:** Believers are encouraged to seek holiness and live as habitations for God's Spirit rather than occasional visitors to His presence. This calling urges us to live a life that reflects His glory and embraces the fullness of His Spirit daily.
- **Holiness as a Requirement for Revival:** Revival and God's glory are tied to holiness, calling believers to uphold their commitment to His righteousness. By living in alignment with His Word, we prepare ourselves to usher in His presence and impact the world.
- **Choosing Between the River or the Sea:** The chapter presents a choice: to live within the river of God's presence or remain in the chaos and uncertainty of life without Him. This choice reflects the path of purpose and fulfillment versus a life lacking divine guidance.
- **A Lifelong Pursuit of God's Glory:** This journey doesn't end with the final page; it is a continuous path of seeking, learning, and living out the truths of His Kingdom. Moving from glory to glory,

believers are called to a constant pursuit of intimacy with God, reflecting His love and light to the world.

Conclusion

As the book closes, the author reminds readers of the life-giving journey they've embarked on, encouraging them to live out the truths learned and press into God's presence. Living in His glory is a lifelong pursuit, one that transforms us and empowers us to shine His light in a world in need. With hearts ablaze and lives surrendered, we are called to remain faithful, eagerly anticipating the day we meet our Savior face to face. Let us run this race with joy and devotion, lifting praise to the One who is worthy of all glory.